GOOD·OLD·DAYS
Christmas
Memories ❄

HOUSE of
WHITE
BIRCHES

PUBLISHERS
SINCE 1947

GOOD·OLD·DAYS
Christmas
Memories

Editor: Ken Tate
Editorial Director: Vivian Rothe

Production Manager: Vicki Macy
Design/Production Artist: Becky Sarasin
Creative Coordinator: Shaun Venish
Production Coordinator: Sandra Ridgway Beres
Production Assistants: Cheryl Lynch, Matthew Martin, Chad Tate,
Janice Tate, Miriam Zacharias
Copy Editor: Läna Schurb

Publishers: Carl H. Muselman, Arthur K. Muselman
Chief Executive Officer: John Robinson
Marketing Director: Scott Moss

Printed in the United States of America
First Printing: 1995
Library of Congress Number: 95-80290
ISBN: 1-882138-16-3

Dear Friends of the Good Old Days,

In all my years with *Good Old Days* magazine, I have had many surprises. Most of those surprises involved tales of ordinary events that, for one reason or another, became extraordinary. The surprise visit of a celebrity in World War II days. The perfect prank played on Halloween tricksters. Box suppers, May Days, Fourths of July—all with almost every conceivable twist of fate.

But Christmas surprises have always been the best! A special gift in Depression days—dreamed of, hoped for, but never expected. The benevolent blessing of a stranger on a crowded city street. All of the special Yuletide meals with families and friends.

Is it any wonder that Christmas memories are the best of the Good Old Days? Christmas has always had a way of softening the hardest times. Somehow Santa always managed to find his way to our homes—and our hearts—bringing with him a beacon of hope when hope often seemed lost.

We were conditioned with stories of love. The love of God, who bestowed his most precious Gift upon the world. The love of wise men who traversed afar in a quest to bestow their gifts of gold, frankincense and myrrh upon the Child born in a stable in Bethlehem. The love of parents who helped us understand the true meaning of the season. The love of grandparents, teachers, neighbors and friends who brought love, peace and joy to those more innocent days.

That is what I have tried to capture for you in the seven chapters and 160 pages of this book. Each story is like a snapshot of our lives—a snapshot I hope will bring a smile, a nod, a sigh of reminiscence to you as you remember those days gone by.

My other hope and prayer is that you will share these stories with someone you love—someone who might be too young to remember Christmas when it was a little less commercial and a little more caring.

I hope you enjoy these stories full of both surprises and love. There will always be good times as long as we have these Christmas Memories of the Good Old Days.

Sincerely,

Ken Tate

Editor

Contents

CHRISTMAS IN THE CITY

CHRISTMAS DOWN HOME

GIFTS OF THE HEART

LIGHTS OF THE SEASON

CHRISTMAS ON THE FRONT

SCHOOL YULETIDE

SEASONS GONE BY

Christmas in the City

Even though we were raised out on the farm, each Christmas Eve we would bundle up for a traditional drive to the nearest town, about 10 miles or so away. There we did our last-minute shopping and afterwards walked and drove our way around the city looking at Christmas lights.

Christmas lights were a novelty to a lot of folks. Those were hard times. Some didn't even have electricity, and many of the lucky ones who had electricity couldn't afford an elaborate Christmas display.

Still, most of the storefronts carried the signs of the seasons. There were rows of brightly colored lights, manger scenes, decorated trees, holly wreaths—all in displays framed by picture windows that were just perfect for a little boy on tiptoes to strain for a look.

My older brother, Dennis, and I would rush from store to store down the bustling walkways, excitedly chattering about all of the sights our young eyes were drinking in. Carolers here and there spiced the frosty air with "God rest ye merry gentlemen …" A Salvation Army group was trumpeting the season—while looking for a few pennies or nickels to help the needy.

Looking in a toy store window and knowing Daddy was nearby, we always ran through an old ritual. First Dennis intoned, "Wow! Looky at that (insert whatever toy we might want for a gift)!" Then I chimed in: "Daddy, do you think Santy Claus could bring us one of those?" Daddy responded: "I don't know. It's been a tough year and Santa has a lot of little boys who would like one."

"Well, what do you s'pose he'll bring us?"

"Oh, a bundle of switches or a lump of coal…" Daddy laughed to let us know it was just a joke.

All around us, other families participated in their own family Christmas rituals of love. And there, on a busy city street, I came to understand a basic truth of life. The spirit of the season simply overpowered the problems of the day. The love of individual families spilled across social and cultural boundaries and—just for a little while—all the love of those families covered the sidewalks and streets just like December's snows.

As you read through the stories which follow, you will join me in fond remembrances of the Good Old Days and Christmas in the city. ✶

—Ken Tate, Editor

A Special Christmas Pageant

By Stan Paregien

"Wally sure messed up the pageant,"
One old woman said as she left the hall.
But most who were there that night
Say it was the best pageant of all.
Wallace Purling was 9 years old,
And retarded, his teachers did say.
That's why he was only in the second grade,
Rather than fourth, on this pageant day.
Kids who were intent on winning
Never wanted Wally on their team.
Often he was left on the sideline,
Waiting, but still able to dream.
Because he was biggest in this class,
He was given the innkeeper's part.
And the teacher helped him practice
Until he knew his few lines by heart.
The night of the Christmas pageant
Finally arrived right on cue.
And all of the second-grade members,
Including Wally, had something to do.
At the appointed time, Joseph and Mary
Knocked on the innkeeper's door.
And Wally, bless his tender heart, said:
"What do you want?" with a roar.

The boy playing Joseph barely squeaked,
"We need a place to spend the night."
Wally barked, "We're full up as usual.
Try the inn down the street, on the right."
Joseph begged, "That inn has no room,
And my wife, Mary, is nearly worn out.
Isn't there a small room or even a stable,
For us to sleep in, here about?"
"No, there is no room in this inn,"
Wally said with a tremble in his voice.
"But, sir," Joseph pleaded, "her baby is due."
That's when Wally's eyes began to get moist.
Wally's voice quivered as he finally said,
"You will have to leave this place."
And as Joseph and Mary turned to go,
The audience saw the tears on Wally's face.
Suddenly, everyone was taken by surprise
As Wally changed his lines to say,
"Wait, please. You can have my room.
You don't have to go away."
Folks still talk about that pageant,
And about what Wally said that year.
Mostly they say the real Christmas spirit
Came through especially loud and clear.

Our Magic Clarinet

By Robert J. Longfellow

The crashing sound of the stock market in 1929, added to the crop-killing drought years to follow, must have aggravated the ugly Great Depression giant. Ultimately, the entire nation collapsed.

During 1933 my parents were desperately fighting to hang on to our farm. But like so many others they didn't make it.

The proceeds from the sale of our equipment, livestock and personal effects went to the mortgage holder and others holding their hands out. Waving goodbye and with tears in our eyes we said farewell to our Kansas farm. With meager possessions we headed for Kansas City, Mo.

Getting settled in a big city was challenging and almost impossible with limited funds. Our grandmother prepared the meals and cared for the small apartment in which all five of us lived. My brother and I entered school and found it dramatically different compared with Stover, our one-room school in Kansas.

My parents pounded the streets for weeks seeking employment. Finally they located work and accepted the ridiculously low wages the jobs paid. They both agreed they were lucky to be on payrolls as there were thousands standing in soup lines having lost it all.

Mother had sacrificed many of her personal possessions to meet the emergencies that arose. We noticed she no longer had her gold watch and other jewelry she had cherished for years.

One evening, a few days before Christmas, we were sitting around the dinner table. A discussion came up regarding the holidays and what not to expect. Grandma said that, as a child in Germany, she was lucky to get a plate with an apple, an orange, a handful of mixed nuts and a homemade toy— usually a rag doll—on it. I thought, *Well this is it. There goes that nifty pocketknife I've dreamed of owning.*

Later that evening, Mother brought out an old instrument case. When she opened it a tarnished clarinet was cradled in the faded, red velvet lining. It had been in the family for years and had formerly been owned by our late Aunt Mayme. Mother figured the sale of it would be the source of our Christmas money … that is, if someone would only make us an offer. We prayed that some kind soul needing a clarinet would soon appear, hopefully before Christmas. Dad said he wondered what the odds would be on that happening.

To improve the instrument's appearance Mother polished the silver parts until they glistened like new. Black shoe polish was applied to the case making it presentable. She brushed out the interior and unsnapped the clip that held the box of extra reeds.

Lifting it out, she gasped, jumped up and let out a squeal of delight. Secured to the bottom was a neatly folded $20 bill. Our prayers had been answered. Who hid it there, and why, will never be known, but to us it was a message from heaven.

I have seen many a Christmas since, but believe me, the one our family had in 1933 will go down in history as the very best! ✶

Christmas in the '30s

By Audrey Carli

How wonderful was that winter day when Daddy hauled in the fragrant evergreen with the bushy branches and prickly needles! What *fun* for parents and children to hang hundreds of shimmering strands on the boughs after Daddy strung the red, blue and green lights. What *joy* to see the cloak of silver illuminated by the multicolored bulbs.

My sisters, brother and I throbbed with the glorious gladness of the season. Santa would visit soon! And we knew the real reason for the season was celebrating Baby Jesus' birthday, and being in the church's program was part of it!

I recall how my Aunt Miriam and I rode the bus to Ironwood every December where we'd shop at the various stores on Main Street. What excitement to walk into the dime store and see the myriad displays of bracelets, games, dolls, and coloring and story books.

There were also puzzles, socks, slippers, gleaming glassware for Mama's kitchen, shining tools for Daddy's workshop.

I recall how my Aunt and I rode the bus to Ironwood every December where we'd shop at the various stores on Main Street.

Baking cookie angels, stars, bells and other holiday-shaped treats marked the season, too. As we helped Mama in the kitchen, cozy from the radiant wood-burning range, the radio filled the room with carols that melted memories into each of us. That's why Aunt Miriam and I talked and planned for cookie baking as we walked from store to store. "Maybe we can find a new cookie cutter to surprise Mama," I said the day I bought her a tree-shaped one.

By the time I'd bought my sister's paper dolls and my brother a coloring book, my dad socks and Mama a hanky (with dimes and nickels saved for months by helping relatives with their newborns and doing other tasks), I searched for my aunt.

I found her and the bulging bag. "Hungry?"

I nodded and we headed for the dime store hot-dog-and-root-beer stand. It was an "island" in front of the store. The air smelled of chopped, raw onions, tangy mustard, spicy ketchup and steaming wieners, warming in a transparent cooker. There was also a container holding soft, fluffy buns which came out warm. What a treat to bite into that hot dog juice with onions and condiments.

The root beer in the thick glass mug fizzed with foam. Bubbles sometimes tingled my nose and engraved delight into my memory.

After that shopping trip, wrapping gifts came next. My best friend and I wrapped presents at her house. She had a room of her own to keep the secret surprises.

Soon it was the evening to get bathed, curl hair and dress for the church Christmas program. The new dresses Grandma sewed for us and the matching hair ribbons were waiting for us.

Long white stockings and patent leather shoes completed the outfits. And when Mama combed and brushed our hair after tossing the metal curlers into a basket, we knew it was truly Christmastime.

Donning our heavy coats, boots, hat and mittens, we trekked down the railroad tracks, across the field and down the street to the white frame church on Pierce Street.

My heart—and many others—hammered while waiting to stand in front of the congregation to recite our "memory verses" about the Bible's Christmas story.

Then we finished reciting and singing, and hurried downstairs. There we were handed treats: popcorn balls and a bag of hard candy with raspberry, lime, pineapple and cherry flavors.

Afterward, we went home and sat around together, gazing at the lighted tree, and heard *Silent Night, Away in a Manger,* and other carols on the brown radio nearby.

On that night, the tree lights looked more brilliant and beautiful than at any other time!

The four of us knelt and prayed, then we each moved a kitchen chair into the room with the tree.

We knew our gifts would be on and beneath them in the morning.

The night was punctuated with fitful, broken sleep. Finally, one sister whispered that even if it was still pitch dark, we should go and check our chairs.

I, the oldest, led the parade to the living room through thick darkness. I stretched out my arms to "feel" the way. I wanted to make sure my fingers touched any object before I bumped into it. Then I clicked on the table lamp, sending brightness over the array of presents. I recall the time I got a sweet-faced baby doll and some storybooks that I read and reread until they were worn and faded.

The day was filled with visits to and from relatives. Delicious food burdened the table. Laughter and gladness swam in the air. As the day waned and a bluish haze covered the snow, another Christmas faded with joy! ✴

Christmas Eve

By Janet McEwen

It was a cold Christmas Eve in my father's dry goods store in Bucyrus, Ohio. Stores did not display Christmas goods months ahead as they do now, but toys and gifts were put out about two weeks before the big day. Nor did stores close at 5 or 6 o'clock on Christmas Eve, as they do now, but remained open until 10:30 or 11 p.m.

It had been a long and busy day, and now it was nearly closing time. Few customers remained and most of the clerks had already left. Business had been good that week, and shelves and cases in the toy department were noticeably depleted of their stock. Dolls had sold particularly well, but a few of the more expensive German-made ones remained.

My father noticed an old woman and little girl at the counter where some of the dolls lay in their cardboard boxes. The woman wore a shawl, the child a thin and ragged coat, small protection from the subzero weather.

He started toward them but was called away by a clerk. As he returned, he saw the woman take one of the largest dolls, and conceal it as best she could under her shawl. On seeing him, she turned her back and, taking the child by the hand, started rapidly toward the door.

He stopped her and said, "Just a minute, Lady. I saw you steal the doll. Now you know you can't do that. I'm sorry, but I will have to

The store owner saw the old woman take one of the largest dolls and conceal it as best she could under her shawl. The old woman and child started to cry. Should he have her arrested? On Christmas Eve?

call the police. It's the law. You just can't do that. I'm sorry."

The old woman started to cry. "Don't do that, Mister," she pleaded. "Please don't call the law. I ain't got no Christmas for the little one. I ain't got nothin'. An' if they lock me up, there ain't nobody to look after the girl. She ain't got no folks. I'm all she's got. I'll give back the doll, just don't send me to no jail."

She handed him the doll. By then the child was crying, too.

"All right," he said. "You can go, but don't ever come in my store again."

As they started to leave, he said. "Little girl, come back here a minute." Eyes large with fright, the youngster slowly came toward him. "Here, Honey," he said, "take the doll. It's a Christmas present from Santa Claus. Merry Christmas!"

Now, you may say my father was wrong; that the child might think, *Even if you get caught stealing, sometimes you get a reward anyway.* Ah, but you don't know my gentle compassionate father. Being the person he was, he could not have done otherwise.

When he told me the story years later, he said, "I thought of my three little girls at home, and of our tree loaded with their gifts from Santa and from our many relatives and friends. It was Christmas Eve, and she was just a little child." ✦

The Corner Christmas

By Donald Skinner

The year was 1934. America was gripped in the clutches of the Depression. The economy lay in ruins, and the unemployed and homeless filled the streets. An air of despair filled every corner of life, and the approaching holiday season loomed bleakly on the horizon.

In a two-room apartment in East Dallas, a mother sat with her two young sons. The oldest boy was 6; the younger was barely 4. They wore patched but clean overalls and shirts. Each had on the one pair of sturdy shoes he possessed. There was food in the apartment, barely adequate, but still sufficient.

The father was away, out of state, on a construction job. One of the few lucky persons to be employed, he nevertheless was sorely tested to maintain two households. The mother knew that this year Christmas must pass her by.

But the looks on the faces of her sons as they passed toy shops or saw the ornaments of the season told her that they believed Christmas would come to them. In her heart and in her mind, she gathered the resolve that somehow, some way, the promise of Christmas would be fulfilled.

Despite the air of despair caused by the Depression, the boys believed Christmas would come to them.

But how? There was no money for presents, ornaments, or even a tree. In her desperate quest, the mother enlisted the aid of her sons. In the spirit of a game, she showed the older one how to cut strips from a brown paper bag. These strips, pasted in circles, linked together to form a chain. Popcorn was popped and, in spite of the younger son's efforts to eat it, was pierced and strung on sewing thread.

In those days cigarette packs contained a layer of metallic foil. Laboriously, bits of foil were peeled off to serve as icicles to drape over the paper and popcorn chains. But there was no tree, so the mother pinned the garlands across a corner of the room. As if decorating a tree, she arranged the paper chains and icicles and declared that, yes, Christmas would come.

As with all children on Christmas Eve, the boys tried to stay up all night. Sleep, however, crept upon them and took them unawares; at last the home was quiet.

But at the dawn, the boys were up, and raced into the front room to view their "tree." The garlands still festooned the corner and the icicles glinted in the first light. But a miracle had happened! For there under the decorations were two apples, two oranges, and two red metal airplanes!

Oh, how the boys reacted when they realized that Santa had indeed found their "tree"! Each clutched his airplane as if it were the grandest thing in the world. No matter that the propellers turned only by hand; no matter that the engines roared only when the boys did. What mattered was that Santa had remembered!

It was many years later that they learned that money intended for a dress to supplement the mother's meager wardrobe had been used at the toy store instead.

The next Christmas was better. The father was back with the family who by now was living on a farm with two other families—one belonging to the father's brother and the other to the mother's sister. The farm at least provided a living, and at Christmas, there was a tree from the woods. Somehow, small gifts were found under the tree, and the red airplanes continued to fly.

Years went by; the economy changed. The family was increased by a daughter. World War II came and went. Each Christmas was warmly celebrated and, during the festivities, someone would mention the "corner Christmas."

The boys eventually left home, the older one to pursue a career as a professor at a major college; the younger one found his calling in the military. The little sister entered the world of business as an accountant. During the infrequent times when all were at home at Christmas together, the "corner Christmas" was remembered. With children and then grandchildren, the family grew larger, and the tale was told and told again.

The father and the older son have since passed on, victims of heart disease and cancer. The mother, lately confined to a wheelchair, lives with and is tended to by the daughter and her family.

The younger son, by now retired and his own family grown, still comes "home" occasionally, but always on Christmas. When the talk turns to other days, and it always does, mother and son still smile as they remember that long-ago day when two boys and a loving mother found that the spirit of Christmas and their love for each other had come to the decorated corner of a bleak apartment room.

There never has been a finer or a grander Christmas.✶

For Unto Us
A Child Is Given

By Verla Mooth

ll through the pre-Christmas days of 1952, our precious 3-year-old son, Dirk, had been asking Santa Claus to bring him a pair of cowboy boots, a gun and holster, a "pickatar" and a baby sister. The "pickatar" was his way of saying he wanted a guitar.

The desire for a baby sister had been planted in his little mind ever since September when he was moved into a twin bed in an effort to prepare him for sharing his life with a new baby.

Our expectations for an addition to our family were based on the fact that the Chicago Foundlings Home, from which we had adopted Dirk as a baby, had informed us that they would have a baby girl for us by Christmas.

Our hearts were filled with joy at the prospect of a second child. We were so fortunate to even be considered for another baby. So many other couples couldn't even get one!

I had redecorated the children's bedroom, making it suitable for both a boy and girl. Dirk's side of the room had a Western motif. On the wall above the baby bed, little rabbits played in clumps of green grass. Both the rabbits and the cowboys had been cut from printed chintz and pasted on the newly painted walls.

Everything was ready. But something seemed to be holding things back. I learned that some of the medical tests I had taken turned out poorly, and I was asked to take them over.

Dec. 22 arrived and we were still waiting. The cowboy boots, gun and holster, the "pickatar" and other toys were gaily wrapped and hidden away for Santa Claus to deliver. But what would we tell our disappointed little boy in case his baby sister did not arrive by Christmas Day? It was a question that filled our minds with anxiety. I started praying in earnest.

To this, add the fact that the winter of 1952 was promising

> *Our hearts were filled with joy at the prospect of adopting a second child. We were so fortunate to even be considered for another baby. So many other couples couldn't even get one!*

to be a severe one. Snow had been falling for most of December and the streets of Chicago were rutted and filled with ice. Even with tire chains, it was almost impossible to travel the streets. The snow was making life so much more difficult!

And then my prayers were answered. The Chicago Foundlings Home called and said we could come see our little girl that day, but we could not take her home until the 24th—Christmas Eve. We were bursting with excitement as we took Dirk down to see our new baby.

She was a precious little girl with fat, chubby cheeks. The nurses lovingly called her Bonnie Butterball, but we had chosen the name Paula. After holding her in my arms, it was difficult to relinquish her for two more days.

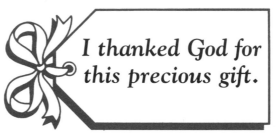

I thanked God for this precious gift.

When the morning of Christmas Eve arrived, everything was prepared to go get our little girl. A bag of baby clothes and a soft, pink blanket were placed in our car.

When we arrived at the Home, there was much excitement. Three babies had been placed in baby seats under the lighted Christmas tree in the old-fashioned parlor. *Chicago News* photographers were taking pictures of the Christmas babies that were to go to their new homes. The pictures were to be featured on the front pages of the various newspapers on Christmas Day. I thought with pride that our little girl was the most beautiful of the three. I am sure the other parents felt the same.

My mother, who was house mother at the Foundlings Home, was coming back with us to spend the Christmas holidays. We thought it best for her to sit in the back and hold the baby so Dirk would not feel pushed aside. It was a slow and difficult trip home, but we finally arrived safely.

My husband's parents were invited for Christmas dinner and to see our new baby. I had lots of work yet to do, but the baby was very fussy in her new home. It was not a good Christmas Eve! I was up all night, and looking out the window, I discovered that it had started to

snow again. By morning, the streets were completely covered. Not one car ventured out. By midmorning, 18 inches of new snow had fallen.

Dirk woke at the crack of dawn and rushed eagerly in to the tree to see what Santa had left him. He was not disappointed. The sound of tearing paper soon revealed that all his requests had been granted.

And there was no doubt about his baby sister being there. Her cry filled the room!

After breakfast, I busied myself with feeding and bathing the baby while my mother put the turkey in the oven. By midmorning the entire house was filled with enticing aromas.

And then the phone rang! It was my mother-in-law. She was crying; my father-in-law refused to venture out in the snowstorm—she wouldn't get to have Christmas or see the baby. To my deep consternation, my husband assured her that he would come after her.

It took two hours to shovel out our driveway and three hours more to make the 10-mile round trip. He lost count of the times he was stuck in the snow. Christmas dinner was much later than planned, but we finally sat down together and gave thanks to God for all his blessings.

The snow finally stopped about noon and the snowplows started clearing the streets. Before dark, my father-in-law decided he would come after my mother-in-law and have some of the leftovers. I was truly happy that my husband would not have to go out again.

By dark, one very tired little boy was ready for bed. He wanted to sleep with his gun and holster and "pickatar." His boots were placed by the side of his bed.

We whispered our prayers, for his baby sister was already asleep. It was the beginning of a lifetime of loving and sharing that is inspiring to behold.

After my mother and my husband had gone to bed, I took advantage of the first quiet moments that I had to be alone all day. I went into the living room where the glowing embers of the fireplace and the lights of the tree were reflecting their shining pattern through the window onto the snow. It was so beautiful!

I felt a deep peace in my heart and my eyes filled with tears of unspeakable gratitude to God for his wonderful gift. I knew that the tiny baby girl who had become ours this Christmas would change our world forever.

I thanked God for this precious gift and I thanked him for the gift of the Christ Child who came to this earth so long ago and likewise changed the world forever.

As the last embers of fire died out, I turned off the lights on the tree and prepared for bed. In the distance I heard the chimes of church bells. Or was it the angels singing, "Glory to God in the highest and peace on earth to men of good will"?

In every fiber of my being, I joined in the sweet refrain: "For unto us a Child is given. Alleluia! Alleluia!" Christmas 1952 is a living memory which brought a gift that grows more priceless with the passing years—a tiny baby girl named Paula. ✷

My Worst Christmas Ever

By Joan Dahlstrom

While reading in my *Good Old Days* recently about the simple loving ways we all enjoyed with friends and family in years gone by, I was reminded of the rapidly accelerating ways of today.

Between the ever-present talk and magazine shows bombarding us, life seems on "fast forward"—complicated and technical. The medical field especially seems to stand out as the pinnacle of change and evolution. I remember when times were different

Christmas Eve of 1949 in Niagara Falls was as anticipated—cold, blustery, almost unfriendly.

All these negatives would have been more than tolerable had I been surrounded by loving family, with the opportunity to enjoy Christmas Eve mass and all the seasonal "perks."

I, however, was a third-year nursing student in a strict Catholic hospital, where, for those on duty, Christmas Eve was no different than a warm July evening. There were patients to care for, routines to follow.

That Christmas Eve I was assigned a large men's ward. I was alone and terribly upset at my rude withdrawal from the arms of a loving family, and of course panic-stricken at the prospect of my huge responsibility.

I carried on quite well throughout the early evening, always fighting off "sorry tears" for myself. I efficiently did all that was expected of me. The sudden, familiar clatter of rosary beads, as the nuns made their rounds, was quite enough to keep me alert and on my toes.

I was especially concerned about Bob, a man of about 45, who had suffered a severe coronary three days before my shift. In those days, there were no intensive care facilities. The full responsibility fell upon the lone nurse on duty. These patients were on total bed rest! No turning, brushing teeth, feeding themselves or even bathing was permitted. To allow them any freedom was to open oneself to the wrath of a nun, which was to be avoided at all costs.

Each patient was enclosed in a plastic oxygen tent that fit

snugly over him, tucked in with a warm bath blanket. The tent was connected to a large oxygen cylinder that seemed to weigh a ton. Now imagine the following scenario!

While making my 10 p.m. rounds—with a much lighter heart at the prospect of my impending vacation—I noticed Bob's oxygen cylinder needed changing. I effortlessly moved the new tank over to his bedside and, wielding a large wrench, began to undo the old tank and connect the new. But I just could not budge the old tank.

Suddenly, I burst into sobs of frustration, and could see that I was visibly upsetting the patient.

With no warning, he suddenly threw back his oxygen tent and jumped briskly onto the cold cement floor with his open hospital gown flapping in the breeze. He muttered, "Why they let you young girls work alone on Christmas Eve with so much responsibility, I'll never know!"

He unceremoniously grabbed the wrench and, with beads of perspiration rolling down his brow, he proceeded to undo the old tank, wrestle the new one closer and successfully open the recalcitrant valve to let the oxygen flow to the tent.

It all unfolded before me like a horror movie.

Bob then jumped back into the bed, pulled the tent over himself and mumbled, "Now go home and have a proper holiday."

I shook from my starched nursing cap to my proper white shoes. To make matters worse, I was too upset to mention the whole sordid affair to my relief nurse.

I went home with a heavy heart and spent the next three days scanning the obituaries, knowing God would take Bob and punish me.

I met Bob about five years later as he was visiting another patient. We embraced and laughed over our shared dark secret. Funny then, but the Christmas of '49 remains my worst ever. ✶

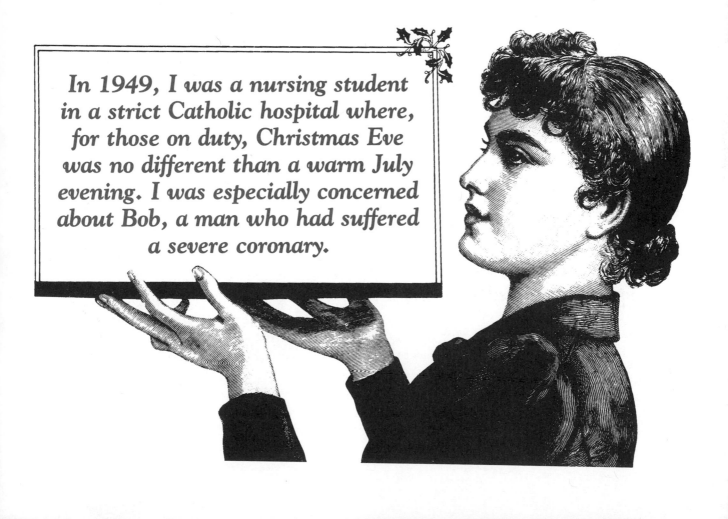

In 1949, I was a nursing student in a strict Catholic hospital where, for those on duty, Christmas Eve was no different than a warm July evening. I was especially concerned about Bob, a man who had suffered a severe coronary.

Christmas B.C.

By R.C. McIntyre

Being born in 1919, I missed the "good old days" of Christmas tree ornaments—strung popped popcorn and live cranberries, plus the fireman's delight—lighted candles in tin clasp holders.

By my early childhood, Christmas tree lights had arrived and the popcorn and cranberries were represented by yards of silver and yards of red glass beads. There were still colored fragile balls which, when dropped, gave all the excitement of a dropped light bulb. There were also life-size birds from Germany and miles of shredded tinfoil representing icicles (aluminum ones hadn't been manufactured as yet).

But it's not the Christmas tree decorations of the Roaring '20s that have stuck in my mind for over 60 years—it's the presents purchased, especially the gift buying for customers if you happened to own a small business.

My dad owned such a small business, a shop dealing in the sale and repair of electric motors, all the way from small ones for washing machines to those 3 feet tall or more found in lumber mills.

For a person with little education, Dad had a thriving business—a double shop, three full-time employees and one part-time, two trucks plus a coupe (a two-door, one-seat auto seating two people) and a catchy name for his shop—"Mac, the Motor Man." He also had a daily 15-minute radio program of recorded music for which my mother wrote the commercials.

There was prosperity after World War I. Business was good. Money was plentiful. And since it kept coming in and you could keep most of it, it was just as plentifully spent, especially at Christmas.

There was prosperity after World War I and we all knew it was going to stay forever.

Business was good. Money was plentiful. And since it kept coming in and you could keep most of it, it was just as plentifully spent, especially at Christmas.

My mother was in charge of purchasing—at least the purchasing of gifts at Christmastime.

Shortly after Thanksgiving, armed with a list of local business people who used my dad's services plus a purse filled with $100 bills, Mother and I sallied forth to help Santa. We sloshed our way from store to store until we finally decided to honor John W. Graham with our purchases.

The excitement of Christmas plus the invigorating eastern Washington December was almost too much for my child-size nervous system. Mother consulted her list, inspected each item and handed over the money. I watched.

It was decided to buy a leather-bound desk blotter, complete with a desk fountain pen in a marble-based holder, for each of Dad's regular customers.

We purchased six sets for $40 each. Bills of the realm piled up on the counter as flakes of snow piled up outside the door.

For the next-best customers, genuine leather billfolds were in order. These were $15 apiece. Four in brown, six in black. Mother insisted that Dad find out what each recipient usually wore so the billfold would complement that color.

The clerk wore an astonished expression when she asked, "How many black billfolds did you say you wanted?" and Mother calmly answered, "Six, please." The floor walker (a constantly walking greeter and security guard—they don't have them now) hurriedly went to the basement to see if they had that many. They did.

Inside each billfold, before they were gift-wrapped, my dad put a crisp $10 bill.

Those customers who were in the third group on the list got leather-covered glass flasks, curved to fit any back hip pocket. This was a daring item in the 1920s as the country officially had Prohibition. The manufacture and sale of any liquor over 1.5 percent alcohol content was illegal. The only available legal liquor was "near beer"—1.5 percent alcohol. (I put in details for those of you too tired to remember or too young to know.)

My dad filled each flask with Canadian whiskey which he got from his rum runner-bootlegger friends, who were also his customers. Flasks were then about $5 each. We

Shortly after Thanksgiving, armed with a list of local business people who used my dad's services plus a purse filled with $100 bills, Mother and I sallied forth to help Santa.

bought 12. I was too young to inquire about the cost of bootleg booze.

Other customers—those who were infrequent callers—received a nicely printed thank-you letter on colorful seasonal stationery in an envelope to match. In the '20s a letter could be mailed for 2 cents.

Our Christmas business was not over. After getting all the gifts home, my mother and I spent many interesting evenings wrapping each item in a different holiday paper with matching ribbons and seals. The wrapping papers had been picked out as carefully as the gifts. No two could be alike. Innovation was the keynote. Scotch tape hadn't been invented so we worked against unruly paper and undisciplined ribbons.

My spindly little fingers held many a ribbon in place while it was being tied and my tongue came out frequently to lick a seal. Mother believed that if a child was born with movable parts they all had a purpose.

The cost of the wrappings was around $25.

It wasn't a one-way Christmas. Give and ye shall receive. We received for days. Many 5-pound boxes of candy and 1-pound fruitcakes piled up under our tree. One year I received three Gilbert Erector sets (interchangeable metal parts plus nuts and bolts which allowed you to make many interesting mechanical items).

Suddenly this joyous, uncontrolled spending came to a stop. October 1929, and the stock market crash started it, although the low point didn't reach the West Coast until about 1932. Christmas gift buying and receiving ceased.

What was taken for granted in the 1920s wasn't possible in the 1930s. Businesses stopped being busy—some went bankrupt. There wasn't enough money for the essentials of daily family living after 1932.

"The good old days," Groucho Marx used say. "May they never come again." Somehow I wish they would. ✶

> *After getting all the gifts home, my mother and I spent many interesting evenings wrapping each item in a different holiday paper with matching ribbons and seals. The wrapping papers had been picked out as carefully as the gifts.*

Christmas in the Rockies

By Bob Langbein

Picture this: It's the Saturday before Christmas, Dec. 19, 1942, to be exact. My folks have given me a late birthday/early Christmas present. It's a Clarion table model radio-phonograph with an automatic changer.

Imagine—30 minutes of 78s without changing, providing the tone arm lifts when one record is finished, and a fresh one drops to replace it.

I'm on the living room sofa with my girl-friend, Marilyn Danhauer. Our glowing Christmas tree lights are the only illumination in the room. The phono is loaded with 10 Glenn Miller ballads. There's a bowl of freshly popped corn and steaming mugs of hot chocolate on the side table.

Fragrances in the room are a wonderful meld of freshly cut pine, popcorn, and Mom's Christmas cookies baking in the kitchen. Looking out the window, we see that God has every intention of giving us a white Christmas as the powdery snow is already covering the ground. What more can a 17-year-old ask of life?

We had moved to Colorado Springs in mid-February of '42, and would live there for the next year while my dad was employed as an architect at the Army's Camp Carson and the Air Force's Peterson Field facilities.

In March I landed a job at Miller's Music Store, George Miller, proprietor. It was here, as a new employee, that my love for the big bands and jazz really took hold. When school ended, I worked full time, and it was then that I persuaded Mr. Miller to order some Commodore records, a slightly more expensive label than those we normally stocked.

"Nobody will pay $1.05 for a 10-inch record, or $1.55 for a 12-inch record of *that* kind of music," Mr. Miller complained.

His preferences were classical, marching band and square dance music, in that order.

Finally relenting, Mr. Miller allowed me to order 25 Commodore records. When the shipment arrived, I sold it out in two days. After that, Miller Music became known as the *jazz* record store. The secret of my success was a large contingent of servicemen, all jazz lovers, all starved for a place to hear and buy the latest recordings.

Among my many customers was one Sergeant Norm Gore, a small-town Iowan, and a walking jazz encyclopedia. We became good friends, and during his off-duty hours, Norm often came to the house for dinner.

On Christmas Day, 1942, the sun was shining upon brand-new white snow. Dad and I hopped into the '37 Packard and drove out to Peterson Field to pick up Norm and a couple of

Looking out the window, we see that God has every intention of giving us a white Christmas as powdery snow falls.

buddies to join us for Christmas dinner. On the way back, we stopped at Victory Lanes and the five of us bowled a couple of games each. Dad picked up the tab. Cost: $2.

Then, it was on to 801 North Weber, where Mom was just beginning to put the food on the table—turkey and dressing and all the other goodies, ending with pumpkin pie. After we all had stuffed ourselves, Norm, his buddies and I went on KP and cleaned the kitchen.

Once finished, we poured some eggnog, put on a stack of records and sat in the living room, our faces glowing from the lights of our tree as we sang with Bing Crosby—*Silent Night, Adeste Fideles, Jingle Bells* and a new song, just introduced for Christmas of '42.

Written for Bing by Irving Berlin, and first sung in the movie *Holiday Inn,* the song we sang that beautiful night, over 50 years ago, was *White Christmas.* ✶

Chapter Two

Christmas Down Home

When I was a youngster, we always cut two Christmas trees. We needed one for us and one for Grandma.

Dennis, Donna and I must have been the luckiest kids on earth. With our widowed grandmother living a short walk away, we had the enviable task of helping to choose, cut and decorate *two* trees and *two* homes.

The only problem with this chore was making a difference between those two trees and two homes, keeping individuality for each.

We usually waited until the Sunday afternoon before Christmas to get our trees. The tiny group of us—Daddy, Mama and three kids—went about our yuletide tasks trooping to the beat of *O Come All Ye Faithful* and *O Little Town of Bethlehem*.

Both trees were chosen from the wooded acreage just across the road from our home. It was a favorite spot of mine, a rough knoll that sloped gently down to a small meadow. The hollows around the pasture were filled with huge oaks, hickories and glade after glade of evergreens.

Daddy had the job of actually cutting down the tree, but he would take a breather long enough for us upstarts to take a hack or two at it. For a long time I just knew that those cedars were part rubber tree the way the ax bounced back from each thrust I made. Dennis always seemed to have better luck than I—but I always figured that it

was because he was five years older. The secrets of woodchopping came much later for this awkward left-hander.

For our home, we usually chose a thick, well-rounded cedar. Dragging it back to the house in the crisp, icy December air, I liked the shape of the cedar and the pungent aroma which filled the living room a short time after trimming the tree. As we hung tinsel and ornaments we laughed and sang together, filled with the spirit of the season.

Then it was off to Grandma's with her tree. Many times I remember us getting Grandma a pine. The pines were sparser of limb, so we had to spend more time planning how we would fill the gaps with various Christmas paraphernalia to give Grandma's tree a little more "body." She always thought the job we grandchildren did was perfect in every way; I think if we had done anything short of burning down the tree with the house around it, the job likewise would have been "perfect" to Grandma.

Finally, it was back to our house for one last round of carols before bedtime. Singing songs of my Maker and his Son filled me with as much warmth as that old wood stove glowing in the corner. Cutting two Christmas trees always seemed to bring twice the fun, twice the love, twice the joy to our little world. That double portion of fun, love and joy always reassured me that at least one season out of the year would be filled with "peace on earth, good will toward men." That was Christmas down home in a time called the Good Old Days. ✱

—Ken Tate, Editor

Merry Christmas

The Little Church

By K.C. Butterworth

The Christmas I remember most fondly was in 1947, and I was 7 years old. Christmas is such a special time of year, and it is the most special time to children. As 7-year-olds do, I had waited all year for Christmas. Little did I know this would be unlike any other Christmas, before or since.

The church my family went to was a little church, and the people who went there didn't have a lot of money. But what was lacking in money was made up in love. Whenever someone was sick, injured, or had a new baby, the ladies brought food, kept their homes running, and did whatever was needed until they could get back on their feet.

Visiting dignitaries always said, "You people are poor in worldly goods, but you are rich in the spirit." And, it was true. As a child, I used to wonder what it would be like to be rich in worldly goods, and not quite so rich in the spirit.

That year was filled with anticipation about the upcoming Christmas program. The congregation was waiting to see how a new minister would handle the program. Each year, Santa Claus arrived at the end of the program, and different ministers handled this in different ways. Some played Santa's part down quite a bit, and some allowed him to have a bigger part in the events. So, this year the new minister would show how he felt about the matter.

There was always a large tree in the church hall, and everyone donated their most prized ornaments to decorate it. Many of the members helped with the preparations, and as the time grew near, the excitement grew. Finally, the day arrived!

As members filed into the hall, I managed to sit close to the front, so the scent from the tree added to my enjoyment of the occasion. As the new minister introduced each number, he interrupted with, "Do I

As Santa rushed through the door, carrying a big bag of gifts, a cheer arose!

hear sleigh bells?" or "Was that a 'Ho, ho, ho!' I heard?" Then he walked to the door, opened it, and peered out, looking for Santa, who didn't arrive until the entire program was completed.

The program consisted of some musical numbers, community singing of carols, and a reading of *The Night Before Christmas*. Throughout the evening, the minister worked us into a frenzy of excitement. By the time Santa arrived, I, along with all the other children, was wide-eyed with excitement.

As Santa rushed through the door, carrying a big bag of gifts, a cheer arose!

The church my family went to was a little church, and the people who went there didn't have a lot of money. But what was lacking in money was made up in love.

Soon I was in line, waiting my turn to sit on Santa's lap, tell him what I wanted for Christmas, and get my Christmas stocking. These were not like the stockings they have now. They were the old-fashioned kind, with holes in them. These were filled with hard candy, nuts and fruit. I can remember how special I felt, taking that stocking home, knowing Santa had filled it especially for me.

This was to be an unusual Christmas program, which was fondly remembered for years to come. There was never another like it. By the

BECKY SARASIN

next Christmas, the new minister had left, and was replaced by yet another new minister.

Many years have come and gone since then. There have been many changes with the passing years. Quite a few ministers have come and gone. The congregation outgrew the little church, and built a big beautiful one. The little church is still standing, but it's no longer a church, it's a lodge hall.

The members have changed also. They are more prosperous, and enjoy a more affluent lifestyle. When people are sick, injured or have a new baby, they rely on their medical insurance for their needs. If more help is needed, they hire it. Visiting dignitaries now say, "You are very blessed to have the money to pay for such a beautiful church."

Now, I sometimes think how wonderful it would be to go back to the little church—to feel the security and warmth in the love that was there. I often feel it might be nice to be a little poorer in worldly goods, but richer in the spirit.

But then I realize that he whose birth Christmas celebrates has given the answer when he said, "Feed the hungry, clothe the naked, care for the sick."

I understand that all the wonderful things I gained in the little church are still with me. All I need do is express them.

And I can do this by following his divine example.

I know that when I'm alone—feeling a little lonely, and maybe a little sad—it's all still there in my mind's eye: the little church, the new minister, Santa with his big bag of gifts and all the feelings of warmth and security. All I need do is close my eyes, think very hard, and I can still see it all. ✳

I sometimes think how wonderful it would be to go back to the little church—to feel the security and warmth in the love that was there.

Christmas Greetings

A Wilderness Christmas

By Nell Parks

No one mentioned wolves, but we all suspected a hungry foe stalked beyond the fringe of forest. Suddenly, frantic yelps and howls split the night.

aiting for a belated city bus, I heard a senior citizen exclaim, "In the old days, we arranged our own transportation any way we could, but we got there on time!"

I recall Christmas week, 1920, when nothing arrived on time except the stork.

I was 10 years old. My father, along with 50 other fathers, worked for a power plant smack in the Canadian wilderness. We lived in company-owned houses and simply referred to our settlement as "camp."

Besides transportation by canoe, snowshoes, dogsled and skis, we could take a company train which ran on a private spur line and meet the Canadian Great Northern train at Lac du Bonnet. Another 65 miles put us in the big city, Winnipeg.

Two weeks before Christmas, Mother announced that I would accompany her to the city. She'd made arrangements for us to stay at the home of a midwife while she kept a date with the stork. Friends would take me to the big stores, she said. I was given the exciting responsibility of buying Christmas presents—Dad's favorite sweetbrier pipe tobacco, Grandpa's chocolate-covered cherries, lavender soap for Grandma. And, I was to find something for 50 cents each for my two brothers who were 6 and 8 years old.

Dad was working shift when we left camp at 8 o'clock, so Grandpa put us on the camp train.

"I hope you get back for Christmas Eve," he said repeatedly, which gave me a nagging worry even the anticipated big-city wonders could not dispel. Christmas Eve in camp meant a real bang-up time in the community hall. I couldn't imagine anything better.

There were millions of footpads in the white forest floor that fled past. Wolves? Deer? Rabbits? A couple of miles from camp, we'd passed the last of the straggling homesteaders' farms. Halfway to Lac du Bonnet, I was surprised to see a curl of smoke coming from an old abandoned trapper's shack.

"Woodcutters took possession there," the conductor informed my mother. "Two men. Bolsheviks."

Russians with whiskers, my mind telegraphed. That winter was unusually severe, which completely stopped construction of any kind. Work was scarce for the hundreds of European men who had preceded their families to make a new home.

At last, we were transferred to the Great Northern's green plush coach.

I whirled around and saw the lamplight coming through a window of the woodcutter's shack. My father muttered, "Thank God."

A week in the city was enough for me. I missed camp activities, my brothers, the wild surroundings I was used to. Would we ever get home? Dad and Grandpa phoned once a day, impatient to know exactly when we'd start home. The stork had obliged by delivering a new sister our second night in the city. Now it was a matter of Mama getting enough strength to travel.

We were again seated in the green plush coach seats. It was the morning of Christmas Eve, mild and thawing. We'd connect with the camp train at Lac du Bonnet about 1 o'clock and be home for Christmas Eve. But my elation thumped to zero when the conductor advised we were running almost two hours late. "Our camp crew won't wait over an hour," Mama predicted unhappily.

She was right. We were stranded in the hotel. "Your grandpa will find a way to get us home tonight," she kept saying through trembling lips as she paced the floor.

I knew she didn't mean to slight my dad. He never took chances with weather or wilderness, whereas Grandpa was famous for being venturesome. "Foolhardy," Dad described it.

Sure enough, they both arrived about 3 o'clock. As soon as Grandpa had seen that we weren't on the camp train, he'd borrowed the section gang's jitney. He was elated because

they'd made good time. Dad was obviously happy to see us, but he reminded us that the morning thaw had turned to ice. The temperature had dropped suddenly. "Perhaps we'd better stay here till morning," he chanced.

"Nonsense!" Grandpa exploded. "This is Christmas Eve, man!"

Dad was still arguing even while he bundled Mama and the new baby, Rosie, and me on the jitney: It'd be dark in two hours; the jitney couldn't get traction on the icy tracks; the camp train would make a special run to get us in the morning.

Mama did a superb job of sounding neutral but siding with Grandpa. Dad looked pretty grim when, at the first incline, he had to get off and push because ice caused the jitney to slip back.

The spur line ran across swampy land which resulted in a year-round battle with uneven track. The worst part was halfway between Lac du Bonnet and camp. We'd skim along for half a mile, then slow to a stop. Both Dad and Grandpa were exhausted from jumping on and off the jitney and pushing. No one mentioned wolves, but we all suspected a hungry foe stalked beyond the fringe of forest. Suddenly, frantic yelps and howls split the night. Our enemy kept just out of sight, except for an occasional dark shadow darting from the trees, then falling back. They'd be still when the jitney was moving, then start howling again when we stopped.

"We'd better stay here the rest of the night," Grandpa announced as if he'd planned it all along.

I whirled around and saw the lamplight coming through a window of the woodcutter's shack. My father muttered, "Thank God." He was talking to himself, and I caught "Never again" when he derailed the jitney and left it where it could be seen. "They'll come looking for us in the morning," he said a little more cheerfully.

Remembering what I'd always been told, that wolves only attack when a human is completely down, I tried to walk very upright in the waist-deep snow to the shack. Grandpa led the way hollering, "Hello, there!" The wolves weren't howling.

Two huge, bewhiskered men filled the doorway and helped us inside. "Ahhh," they uttered with concern. Apologetically, they showed Mama two bunks where she might lay the baby down—two rough log bunks with planks covered with newspapers. It shocked me to know they had no bedclothes but covered themselves with their heavy winter coats. Their stove was an old drum set in rocks and cement with a length of stovepipe. At least there was no shortage of wood. Some nail kegs for seats and an unpainted table made up all the furnishings.

Our hosts busied themselves like two housewives and brewed tea. They offered dark, hard bread.

"Is that all they have to eat?" I whispered.

Grandpa managed to explain that they probably had venison cached away but were afraid to offer it. No doubt it had been shot out of season and they weren't sure who he and Dad might be.

Rough in appearance, but gentle, the men made a great to-do over the baby and me. In limited English they conveyed that they, too, had children in the Old Country. We felt their loneliness. As they tried to carry on a conversation, it was plain the new land had offered them little so far, and their hopes were at zero for an early reunion with their families.

After awhile, Mama lay down beside me and the baby. Dad and Grandpa sat at the table talking to the Russians. "Plenty of work in the spring," Grandpa assured them. "Look me up. I'll help you get started."

Dad rummaged through our suitcases and found his prized tobacco. "Help yourselves. It's for you," he said, smiling for the first time.

Grandpa asked if we'd brought his chocolates and passed them around too.

Missing Christmas Eve in the camp was no longer a gnawing regret. I finally fell asleep with a thought that our arrival at the shack had been planned by a mysterious Christmas spirit.

Tomorrow, Grandpa and Dad would get a dogsled and bring a hamper of food to the men—Christmas cake and mince pies, some fresh fruit, maybe a bottle of Grandpa's blueberry wine. Most of all, they'd bring themselves and some encouragement to our melancholy, despairing hosts.

I've never since spent a Christmas Eve so devoid of all the traditional trimmings and old friends, yet so satisfying. It has stayed with me for more than 50 years. ✷

A Cabbage Rose Christmas

By Donna Dailey

he raindrops plinking on the tin roof made a comfortable sound. From their breakfast table Wil and Luella stared through the steamy kitchen window, sipping their coffee in silence. For three days and three nights the rain had not stopped.

Wil said, "That's the end of the haying for this year. When the rain stops we'll finish what little harvest there is."

The rain finally ceased, but it had been a bad year for crops with too much rain the whole summer. They dug the potatoes, throwing away the rotting ones. "Hardly worth fooling with," Wil said. But they had to put by everything possible for the winter months ahead. They picked the green tomatoes left on the vines and that was the end of their harvest for this year—a disappointingly meager one.

Winter came early and Christmas approached with little hope of special gifts for the children. Luella searched her mind for Christmas gifts for 7-year-old Louise and 12-year-old Libby. She prayed for an answer to her dilemma but the day before Christmas came and there were still no gifts for the girls. Luella had made a rag doll for 3-year-old Blanche and Wil was making something for the boys.

Before the children came home from school, a buggy pulled into the lane. It was their neighbor, Henry. "I picked up a package in town for you, thought it might be important," Henry said.

Luella recognized her mother's handwriting and tore the package open. "It's the answer to my prayer!" She exclaimed. "Material to make dresses for the girls."

"They had oranges and bananas at the store so I brought you a Christmas treat and Emma sent a turkey. She raised them this year and saved one for you," Henry said.

"Oh, Henry, you are an angel! How can we ever repay you?"

"Luella, you don't owe us anything," Henry said. "You've helped Emma with the birthing of our babies and you're always there when we need you. I know you're anxious to get started on that material, so I'll be heading back."

Luella set to work immediately on the dresses. When the children came home from school, Wil hitched the horse to the sled and said,

"Climb on and we'll go to the woods to get the Christmas tree."

In the woods there was much discussion over which tree would be best. When they finally agreed, Wil cut it down with his ax and placed it on the sled. The horse's harness bells rang out merrily as the sled glided over the soft snow.

When they got home they put the tree in the living room. Luella had supper on the table and they ate and hurried with the dishes so they could decorate the tree. There were mounds of popcorn to be strung, a box of pretty buttons, pinecones, strands of paper rings and gingerbread men to hang. After decorating the tree they stood back and gazed in awe at the beauty they had created. The children were rushed off to bed and Luella continued sewing throughout the night.

It was Christmas Eve, and there were no gifts for the children.

When Christmas morning came, the house was alive with laughter and excitement. Luella had put the turkey in the oven sometime during the night and the delicious aroma of roast turkey filled the house. There was a bowl of homemade candy for each child. Their stockings, which they had carefully hung on the mantle the night before, each bulged with an orange and a banana.

Little Blanche hugged her rag doll, rocking it back and forth and chattering happily.

Wil had cut two heavy, narrow strips of leather, and put a hook at the end of each to make razor strops for the boys. It made Dutch, 14, and Carl, 16, feel grown-up to sharpen their razors with their own strops.

Libby and Louise danced around the room in their new dresses. They had made a present for Ma by cutting two small squares of wool, stitching them together and stuffing it with hair which they had collected from their hairbrush. Libby decorated the edges with lace and it made a pretty pincushion; the hair would keep Ma's pins and needles sharp and unrusted. They had knitted warm mittens for Pa.

Luella had saved large, empty tin cans, tied them together tightly and put a soft padding on the top. She covered them with heavy ticking and then knitted a cover to make a footstool for Wil to rest his feet on in the evenings.

Wil gave Luella a square wooden box on which he had carved flowers and leaves. When she opened the hinged lid, there was the most beautiful scent of roses. "Oh, those sweet-smelling cabbage roses!" she exclaimed. During the summer Wil had collected the rose petals from her garden, dried them, and put them in the box for her.

"If you leave the lid open," he said, "the whole room will smell like roses. I thought you might like to smell them in the winter, too."

Luella could not have asked for a present that would have pleased her more. The fragrance of the roses drifted through the room, filling it with an aroma which matched the love that abounded on this day—so much love that it made up for all the things they lacked.

Soon Luella would have to start cooking the big Christmas dinner, for there would be many relatives arriving to share the day with them. But for now she wanted to pause and take in the beauty of this moment—the aroma of the roasting turkey, the exquisite perfume of the rose petals and the excited laughter of their children.

She took Wil's hand and pressed it to her cheek. She could hardly contain all the love she felt in her heart. It was full and spilling over, transcending all the sorrow and hard times they had known. Sweet memories flooded Luella's thoughts and in her mind's eye she could see her mom's little rose garden and the rose bushes started from Grandma Lavina's bush.

In 1883, Luella and her parents moved into a log cabin built by her father. One of the first things her mother did was to start a rose garden. And when Luella married she had a "start" from the same rose bush. What a perfect symbol of love was this cabbage rose—a symbol of love which she would pass on to her own children.

That's what Christmas is all about, Luella thought, *remembering, loving and sharing. Remembering the birth of Jesus, remembering each other. God passed his love to us with the gift of his Son and we, in turn, pass love to each other—generation after generation—in a never-ending thread.* ✳

Christmas In the Foothills

By Hannah E. Lords

t was not a matter of calling for a moving van and "leaving the moving to us" when Mary Lords and eight of her nine children moved from Pocatello, Idaho, to Bynum, Mont., in late December of 1927.

They had two Model T Fords; one, a truck with a 6-by-10–foot box built on the back and the other, a touring car with snap-on isinglass windows. A home-built trailer was pulled behind this vehicle, except on the steeper hills where it was necessary for both vehicles to be turned around and backed up the hill. In that case the trailer was hooked onto the front of the touring car and they ascended the hills in that fashion. Some roads were graveled but many were picked earth. We would call them back roads or even trails today, but they were the only roads at the time.

The oldest family members looked forward to their destination with hope and enthusiasm. The family had suffered much deprivation since the loss of their father two years earlier. Now their local church had found them this new opportunity to sharecrop on 160 acres of irrigated land in the foothills of the Rockies. It seemed like a dream come true.

But not for the smaller members of the family. For 5-year-old Mearl, 7-year-old Bill and 9-year-old Clarence it was the worst thing that could happen. There were only six days before Christmas and they had a sinking feeling that Santa Claus would not be able to find them in that faraway place to which they were going. The prospect of a better living seemed a distant thing compared to the immediacy of their present situation. It was unlikely there would be any cause for rejoicing this year.

As one day on the road followed another the boys wondered if they would even arrive at their destination in time for Christmas. Their older sister, Lottie, 11, tried to keep them amused, but being confined to the two vehicles in close proximity to one another was trying for the energetic boys who were used to running through the countryside unhampered by time or distance.

Now their thoughts centered on old freedoms, their losses, and the frustration of facing an unidentified future.

Every morning at first light they were rousted out of their cramped sleeping places amongst the household items and sent to find an uninhabited bush. When they emerged, they ate a cold and hurried breakfast of bread and whatever else Mom could find. Then they hit the road again. Except for brief stops to meet their most desperate needs, or those of the other vehicle, they drove, drove and drove until well after dark.

With everyone now eagerly looking forward to freedom from their life on wheels, they found themselves delayed in a pitch-black night by a blinking light at a country railroad crossing.

At first it was good to take advantage of the

"Santa Claus will surely not be able to find us now. We must have drove a zillion miles."

stop to stretch aching muscles. But as they waited and waited and were only met with the blackness and silence of the night they finally became irritable and cross. It seemed like a good time to air all the frustration and anger pent up by the insecurities of moving, the lifting, tugging, decision-making ("Does this go? Is there room for that?") and the ever-present question: "Will this move enhance our lot in life or destroy it?"

From the oldest to the youngest they all felt these questions arise as they were held at bay in the dark night by a sign forbidding them to cross and get on with their journey.

Finally the oldest boy, 19-year-old James, walked up to the tracks shining in the car lights. Getting down on his hands and knees he laid his ear against the track. Lifting his head after a while he looked up and down the rails, then he laid his other ear against the track. After a few seconds he rose and walked toward the waiting family, his face a doleful mask in the car lights as he approached.

"There ain't no train. That signal is just stuck," he said and, with a shake of his head, he slipped behind the wheel of the truck and drove across the empty track.

A sense of bewilderment clung to their hearts and minds as they drove on. Was there an arm of the law waiting out in the dark ready to pounce on those who did not heed the flashing light? But what about their embarrassment in being delayed for a purpose that did not exist? Weariness covered them like a shroud. No longer was it just the young ones who moaned and groaned over the cold and length of days. This trip was taking much longer than they expected. They were all tired of living in the cold.

And so it was late Christmas Eve when they finally pulled to a stop at the rambling, cold-looking, big house that was now to be their home. Immediately the oldest children sprang into action. Under their mother's direction Jesse, 13, Roy, 15, and Dewey, 17, along with Lottie and James, made up beds for the three younger boys in an upstairs bedroom. Then with the door tightly closed against the noise and confusion, they went about unpacking the vehicles and trailer.

Though they had not encountered any snow on their trip, the air and their bedclothes were crisp and cold in the wintry night of the foothills. The young boys snuggled down and waited for the precious warmth of their bodies to include the bedding.

"Santa Claus will surely not be able to find us now," said Bill sadly. "We must of drove a zillion miles."

"And he sure can't come down that little skinny stovepipe hole," Mearl added, remembering the big heater he had glimpsed in a large room off the hall downstairs. Fatigue ended further pursuit of such concerns when sleep overtook them.

Christmas morning dawned and Clarence woke the others to explain that they could now stretch their full length. No longer was it necessary to curl in whatever places they could wedge their bodies in the bouncing box of the truck. And it was warm! They hadn't been warm since they left their home in Idaho six days earlier.

Throwing back the covers they were delighted to find it remained warm, even without the covers! To further their joy they opened the door and looked down the stairs. It was still warm! They ran downstairs to a big room they had not been able to see in the dark the night before. Standing in the corner of the large room was a tall Christmas tree, fully decorated! Under the tree was a stack of brightly colored boxes tied with bright red and green ribbons and bows.

The boys stood back, eyeing the tree in speechless wonder. Then they ran in search of their mother. They found her in the kitchen behind a mound of food. A fully cooked turkey and all the fixings sat on the long kitchen counter. Surrounding it were cakes, pies, pickles, apples, oranges and even nuts and candy! Could they be dreaming? How could this be?

"Did Santa bring all this? How did he find us?" Bill asked.

When they ran out of questions and finally stopped, their mother pulled them close and explained. "Our neighbors, the wonderful people of the church and this community, have gotten together and done all this for us!" The mother and children stared at each other, caught up in the magic and wonder of this never-to-be-forgotten Christmas.

Now the boys are grown men themselves, but they never forget to tell their grandchildren and great-grandchildren of that first wonderful Christmas in a very small town called Bynum, Mont. ... the *living* Christmas, portrayed by the church and community who, though they had so little themselves, were still willing to share that little with this hurting family. ✴

Coal-Mining Christmas

By Juanita Perret

I grew up on a farm in the coal-mining country of the South where money was a luxury. Christmas was a tree from the hillside decorated with homemade trimmings, and dinner whatever meat, vegetables and canned fruits we had. Anything store-bought was a treat.

The youngest in the family sometimes was lucky enough to receive a wagon or a tricycle and the rest of us shared a bag of candy or nuts. My mother, a devoted Christian, taught us the meaning of Christmas is the celebration of Christ's birthday and not necessarily the bounty of gifts received.

One Christmas, Dad gave each of us $1 to spend as we wished. After considerable deliberation with my four brothers, we decided to spend the money on our mother.

With the country store three miles from home his destination and his legs for transportation, my oldest brother, designated shopper, was on his way with specific instructions on the purchase.

In a few hours he returned with the largest waste basket we'd ever seen, filled with chocolate candy, bananas, citrus fruit and mixed nuts—all the "goodies" we loved, but could never afford. The excitement mounting, we hid our surprise in the smokehouse and covered it with burlap bags to keep it from freezing.

When we presented the basket to Mom, she had tears in her eyes and told use we were the best kids in the world. Then, with our ever-present enthusiasm, we all shared one big Christmas gift together.

It has been a few years since I spent Christmas at home, but the true meaning of Christmas will remain with me the rest of my life. That day, though the exact date is long forgotten, truly is my most memorable Christmas. ✴

Home for Christmas

By Marie Wells

riday afternoon, December 1923, the Christmas entertainment was over. The tree with its decorations of paper chains, silvery stars, snowflakes and other creations inspired by the children's Christmas spirit stood bare of gifts—a has-been! I, the teacher in that one-room Nova Scotian rural school, viewed the thickening snowstorm with consternation; the children, with anticipation.

Finally, clutching their gifts, the remaining helpers sang once more, "Jingle bells, Jingle bells, Jingle all the way …," chorused a "Merry, merry Christmas" and started home.

> ## The thought of not getting home for Christmas seemed a major disaster.

The last chore done, I locked the door and trudged wearily back through the falling snow to my boarding place, the home of my mother's cousin. After the family supper, I helped with the dishes, put a few more things in my partially packed bag, and tried to read. The hours dragged by as the wind whistled and the snow whirled against the windows. At last bedtime came; finally sleep shut out my desolation.

Saturday morning and no road in sight; some of the windows were almost covered by banks of snow—but the storm was over. It was five miles to the railroad station in Amherst. Could the roads be broken in time? The lump in my throat made it hard to swallow Cousin Ida's good farm breakfast. The thought of not getting home for Christmas seemed a major disaster.

The barn work done, Cousin Edgar and son were opening a path down the long lane. Minutes seemed hours as I watched for the road-breaking crew. Could they possibly get it opened in time for me to catch the train five miles away?

At long last, or so it seemed, came the teams of horses harnessed to bobsleds, and the men with shovels. Here and there the horses could plunge through the snow, as their drivers urged them on. When they came to a halt, the men went to work with their shovels, then another advance, then another bank. At last the crew had gone from sight. Time dragged on!

Clapping his cold hands and stamping off the snow, Cousin Edgar finally came in, expressing his sentiments in his usual warm vocabulary.

"Well, young lady, we'll try it. If the train is late, and it will be, we might make it."

It did not take me long to get into my things. Cousin Ida handed me my lunch; Greta wrapped the hot brick for the sleigh; Cousin Edgar took my bag. With a last "Merry Christmas," I tucked the buffalo robe around me and put my mittened hands into my fur muff. Cousin Edgar shook the reins and Dinah started off, shaking her long string of bells, but rarely could she break into a trot.

My Waltham watch soon told me that it was time for my train, though we were still three miles away. We finally reached upper Victoria Street, where many of Amherst's well-to-do were housed. Here, tired Dinah was urged into a trot. Soon the station came in view—and there stood the train! Would it wait until I got my ticket? Tension mounted! I grabbed my bag, said a hurried goodbye, and ran.

"All aboard," came the call. I hesitated; the conductor beckoned. I climbed the steps, was handed my bag, and collapsed into one of the few remaining seats. The day coach from Montreal was redolent with the smell of oranges, packed lunches and tired people.

The conductor gave me a ticket. The train crept forward over the icy tracks—Maccan, Nappan, Springhill Junction (a long stop for water), Salt Springs—Oxford Junction! There awaited our little shortline train.

Now I knew I'd get to Pugwash, but what would I do if my father could not make the six miles from our farm at Wallace Bay?

"Pugwash, next stop," the conductor finally called, as the train inched around the bend. It was hours late and it was pitch-dark. I was first in line to get off the train. The kindly conductor helped me down.

My heart sank as I walked toward the station, but at the car ahead I saw a tall shadow. There was my father! He helped me into the old 'coon coat, the winter extra wrap for returning daughters. No one-horse sleigh awaited me, but Ned and Doll, harnessed to the bobsled. There was still a bit of warmth in the once-hot bricks.

Again a buffalo robe was tucked in and off we started. Away from town progress was slow, the road frequently wending its way through the fields to avoid the banks of snow. As we came down our marsh, a few stars ventured out of the dark sky, and a shadowy moon appeared. The light through the kitchen window from the lamp sent out its welcome.

Soon the family was out in the wintry night to greet me, the dog wagging his tail, a brother taking my bag, Mother saying, "Come in. You must be starved." I had made it home for Christmas.

The black range glowed with burning wood as I passed through the family kitchen. The tall balsam tree waited in the corner of the "sitting room" which, as always on Christmas, was decked with boughs and with streamers attached to the central hanging lamp. The old Franklin with its wide chimney, down which Santa used to slide, was ready with backlog and kindling. The fire in the hall stove had broken the chill of the upstairs. I quickly removed my outer wraps, and a tired but happy and hungry daughter joined a hungry family for the belated meal. ✳

A Grandmother's Story

By Nova McCurdy Lee

Grandfather was the storyteller for his grandchildren, but there was one story Grandmother felt we should hear and she knew he would never tell it, for Grandfather was not a boastful man.

There had been a drought in the valley one year and every family was hit hard. A late frost killed the fruit, and what gardens were planted—because there had been little rain during the winter—failed.

Sometime during the year, Grandfather had bought lumber and red paint and planned to build a better barn. But when things got worse, he had to take a job in Mr. Bently's blacksmith shop to help feed the family.

"Your grandfather was a good man with tools," Grandmother said. "And plows had to be sharpened and horses shod, so he and Mr. Bently were kept busy even though most of it was done and they had to wait on the pay."

Grandmother remembered how a few folks had to sell pigs and even their milk cows to buy food and make the mortgage payment. The ones who had the most sold cattle so they could help out old people or younger ones who were "just setting up housekeeping."

"Those were hard times," she said. "Mighty hard." And taking it all the way around, it was much worse than they thought it could be. "But the people had a strong faith and little complaining was heard."

Somehow they managed to get through the spring and summer, but when autumn came their spirits had waned somewhat.

"There was winter coming on," Grandmother said, "and about the only thing we had left was enough wood to keep us warm."

While most of the people were wondering how they were going to make it until another year, Grandfather, it seemed, was thinking of something else. He was concerned about what was going to happen to those children in the valley come Christmas Eve when there would be no toys from Santa.

"It bothered your grandfather a heap," she said. "There were 18 boys and 15 little girls. That's a lot of children when there is no money to buy gifts."

Grandfather had been confronted with many problems in his lifetime, but this was one for which he didn't seem to have an answer. "You know," Grandmother told us, "I don't think I ever saw a man worry so much. 'Ellen,' he said to me, 'we can't let those children go through Christmas without any toys. They would never believe in Santa again.' And by now I had commenced to feel the same way."

It seemed that Grandfather spent night after night—when the family was in bed—sitting by the fireside, racking his brain and trying to think of some way to keep those boys and girls, including his own, from being disappointed Christmas Eve.

Grandmother smiled, then went on. "Your grandfather is a good man with a big heart." So with his thinking and pondering he was bound to come up with an answer, and he did. His solution to the problem made every child—the older ones as well—forget the hardships they had endured through the year, and joy filled their hearts when Christmas came

"That was a Christmas that I think every one of those youngsters remembers to this very day," Grandmother said. "It must have been the biggest surprise they ever had."

The new lumber and red paint Grandfather had bought to build the barn solved the problem. With Grandfather's help, they went to work on a project that took weeks to complete.

Fortunately he was still helping Mr. Bently in the blacksmith shop a few days a week and this gave him access to tools he did not have at home. He counted the number of sleds and doll cradles they needed and selected lumber, picking out the best pieces.

"Your grand-father thought he would still have enough lumber left to build a small granary," Grandmother said, "but the

more he thought about his plan, the more excited he became and more toys to build were added to the list."

Wagons could be built and even rocking horses for the small tots. There was no limit to the doll furniture that could be made, and if Grandmother would do some sewing, maybe they could take the little girls' old dolls and dress them up in new clothing.

"So," Grandmother said, "I began planning about what I'd do—we would need little mattresses, pillows and quilts for the doll cradles as well."

Why, they both told each other, this could turn out to be the most exciting Christmas the valley had ever had. But Grandfather was a wise man who knew his neighbors. He had had similar experiences with them before and knew they were not the kind of people who would accept charity.

This project could not be done by himself and Grandmother alone. He would have to work it out so every family would have a hand in it and feel they were doing their share. It would have to be a community project.

So, he saddled up old Bertha and paid a visit to every neighbor, going at a time when the older children would be in school and those at home

"We can't let those children go through Christmas without any toys. They would never believe in Santa again!"

were either too young to understand or would be taking a nap.

The people in the valley liked Grandfather and respected him. He was a man who knew how to talk to people, and had given a lot of thought to his plan. So he presented it in such a way that it made them almost feel it had been their idea to begin with.

"I'll tell you," Grandmother said proudly, "when they learned they were included they took to the idea like mice after a hunk of cheese."

The menfolk were to help Grandfather with the toymaking and the women would join Grandmother in sewing and knitting. The older boys and girls had to have gifts as well. There'd be socks, mittens, stocking-leg caps and mufflers.

There was no limit to what could be made. Wagons could be built, and even rocking horses for the small children.

"Gather up all the wheels you can find," Grandfather told Mr. Tyler's hired hand. "We'll need them for the wagons we are going to build."

"Your grandfather is a man who believes in doing things right," Grandmother said, "so he asked each family to make a list of the things they would buy for the children if they could afford it."

It was agreed that the work would be done at Grandfather's house for he had a workshop. Then, things he needed to take in to the blacksmith shop would be handy when he went in.

"And the women came there to work, too," Grandmother said. "I had a big box for quilts and we could hide what we were working on every day when it was time to stop." Then all of Grandfather's and Grandmother's kids were in school so there would not be any questions to answer.

It turned into a wonderful neighborhood project and everyone worked with fine spirits, forgetting the adversity of the year which was now behind them.

The work began around the last week in November. They had to start early so the paint would have time to dry. While the menfolk worked on toys, Grandmother and the women of the valley made doll clothes (every mother had gathered up her little daughter's old doll so new clothes could be made for it), mattresses, pillows and pieced doll quilts.

"It was more fun than we ever had at a quilting party," Grandmother recalled, "for we were doing something to make our children happy and keep them from being disappointed when Santa didn't come."

Grandmother waited awhile, a smile on her lips as though remembering the good times they had. Then she said, "We had bits of lace, insertion, crochet and ribbons scattered here and there."

Grandfather drew up plans for the toys and he and Mr. Bently made the runners for the sleds. Mr. Bently had no family except a wife and one grown son. "But I never seen a man get so caught up in the spirit," Grandmother said. He agreed to furnish all the nails, screws, bolts or anything else in his shop they might need.

"That plan of your grandfather's brought the valley people closer together than they had been for a long time," Grandmother told us. "And it helped us all to forget the hard times we had gone through."

As they moved into December, the weather turned bad and they all went to Mr. Bently's blacksmith shop to work. "The warmth from that forge sure helped out," Grandfather said.

But the men were so carried away with their work no one seemed to mind having to drive home over icy roads or in a snowstorm. The womenfolk made lunches for them to take each day so they could spend as much time working as possible.

After the toys were all built, the painting began. The only color Grandfather had was the red paint he had bought for the barn, but the other men brought in paint they had leftover from doing odd jobs around the house and Mr. Bently felt so bighearted he bought a bucket of green paint.

"My!" Grandmother said. "How pretty those toys were when the menfolk brought them home. There were red wagons with yellow and green wheels, red and green sleds with yellow stripes, and the rocking horses were bright red with yellow noses and green eyes."

If they had light-colored paint, this was used for the doll furniture, but even some of that had to be painted red or green with trim of another color.

Both Grandfather and Mr. Bently were good with ironwork. The runners that came up in front of the sleds were formed like the neck of a swan, then smoothed down and skillfully painted.

Two weeks before Christmas everything was ready—every single toy had been built and painted. Grandmother and the ladies had completed their tasks and old dolls wore fancy dresses; little mattresses, pillows and patchwork quilts were ready to be put into cradles. Gifts for the older boys and girls had been knitted from bright yarn.

So the toys were brought home and everything that could be wrapped was done up in white paper—some had saved colored paper they had taken from wrappings that came from the store—and tied with red string. This, too, had been saved all year.

The sleds, wagons, rocking horses and much of the doll furniture could not be wrapped, so tags were cut and the child's name written on it. Then the tag was tied to the gift he would receive.

It was decided the tree would be at Grandfather's house since the toys would be difficult to take to the church. "We can go there for awhile," Grandfather told them, "and let the children put on their program as usual. Then after we sing, the parson can give a talk and prayer."

This idea pleased everyone, for they realized the toys had to be kept out of sight. (Young eyes usually did a lot of snooping at this season.) So the large toys were hidden in the cellar and covered with a piece of canvas. Grandmother managed to hide the other packages under the bed and in her big quilt box.

"Once Lucy almost discovered a box of things she was not supposed to see until Christmas," Grandmother told us. "Maybe she had begun to get suspicious like children do near Christmas. I told her it was scraps I was saving to make a couple of comforters for the beds."

Three gifts were especially unselfish.

"Two of the young ladies were to be married in the spring," Grandmother said, "so I tore up my wedding dress and made three fancy petticoats." (One was for little Lucy.)

"I trimmed them in lace and ribbons, but before I finished the last one, I ran out of lace and had to use three different kinds. I knew Lucy was too young to mind so I gave it to her."

When Christmas Eve arrived everyone went to the church as planned. "We told the children that, since it had been such a hard year, we were making it easy on Santa. And, if we had the tree at our house, he would not have so far to come."

There were a couple of bachelors who worked as hired hands, and they agreed to stay at Grandfather's and put up the tree and decorate it while the others were at church.

"We womenfolk had baked cookies and made molasses candy and we had strings of popcorn for the tree." The men knew the larger toys were in the cellar, but when everyone was out of the house, Grandmother pretended she had forgotten her gloves and went back inside. "The men knew about the toys in the cellar but I had to drag those out from under the bed and get the gifts out of the quilt box."

The children had seemed a little disappointed at going to the church and not having a tree, but they were all told there would be a tree at Grandfather's when they got back.

It must have been an excited group of children when they walked through the parlor door at Grandfather's and Grandmother's house and saw that big tree waiting. The men had built a fire in the old potbellied stove and one of the men was there to have the door open while the other had put on the red suit and was waiting outside until everyone got in the house.

As soon as the door closed, there was a jingle of bells and in came Santa, waving and calling out, "Merry Christmas!"

"Those younguns' eyes popped out like they'd seen a ghost," Grandmother said. "They knew it had been a poor year, and while they expected Santa to bring something, they had not expected anything like what they saw."

The two men had done a good job at trimming the tree. The paper chains had been used so many times they would hardly hold together, but no one noticed. Cookies and candy (and fruit the bachelors had bought for their contribution) hung by strings on almost every branch.

The candles in their metal holders had been used year after year; each Christmas they were a little shorter, but still gave off some light. Together with the kerosene lamps and glow of the fire through the isinglass, there was nothing

Never had there been such a Christmas in the valley! People were laughing and talking as though it had been a prosperous year.

on that tree or under it that was missed by the eyes of those children.

Never had there been such a Christmas in the valley! People were laughing and talking as though it had been a prosperous year. The drought, the failure of crops and lack of money were all forgotten.

"I don't think I've ever seen a man as happy as your grandfather was," Grandmother said. "He watched those children tearing away paper and hugging toys and the smiles on the faces of those who got sleds and wagons, and I believe he felt like a child again himself."

It was a lot of happy neighbors who loaded the gifts and went home that long-ago night (after being served gingerbread, pumpkin pie and coffee). When the door closed on the last sled and doll cradle, Grandfather and Grandmother must have looked at each other and known in that moment the true meaning of "Peace on Earth and goodwill toward men." ✳

Christmas Past

By Leota Kuykendall

y memories of Christmases past contain basic values that laid the foundation for my life. Our rural German family maintained old customs and stayed isolated from the greater community until well after World War II. I was born into this family in the mid-'30s, at the threshold of change. Christmas memories are among my most cherished from those times.

At our house Christmas began at 4 p.m. sharp on Christmas Eve. We kids all had bathed and shampooed and eaten our supper by that point. My mother told us kids to go watch for Santa to come. It was 4 o'clock, and if we didn't watch close, we would miss him. As she prodded us from behind, we pressed our noses to the cold, wet glass and stared intently up the road along the fencerow, looking for Santa.

All of a sudden my mother would change her tone and laugh, telling us we'd missed Santa again. He was already gone! (What an experience it was, the first year I found myself in front of that window knowing there wasn't a real Santa Claus, while all my younger siblings stared out the window, intently still believing in Santa.)

Turning from the window, there behind us we would see the Christmas tree. In those moments while we had been staring out the window, Santa had tossed the gifts under the tree. We'd run for the gifts and enjoy them for a few minutes.

The gifts were always the same. There was a new rubber doll with new doll clothes for the girls. (My mother sewed the doll clothes.) My brother got a truck. The girls each received a new dress with new socks. The dresses were made by my mother from feed sacks. Store-bought items came straight from the Sears or Montgomery Ward catalog. Sometimes Daddy complained about the size of the bill for that catalog order, but every year the order came.

There wasn't much time, so soon we had to lay down the dolls and wait to play later. We had to hurry to get to the Christmas Eve program. Into those new dresses and socks! The program was always the same. The children played out the Christmas story, dressed as angels, shepherds, wise men, Mary and Joseph, with a doll in the manger for Baby Jesus.

I do not recall playing any particular parts in the plays except readings. Once I was given a very long reading. At my young age I worked hard and long to memorize it. On that Christmas long ago when

I recited the verse, I recall secretly feeling pleased to have learned such a long verse. Positive compliments were not a part of my upbringing so I held my pride in secret. We also learned to sing *Away in a Manger* and other carols, all in the German language of my early childhood years.

After the program, a rattling noise came from the back of the church where the deacons were moving paper sacks around. Up front a deacon would read the names of individual families from a list, followed by the number of members in that family. I always wondered if our name would be called. It was hard for Daddy to pay for the paper sacks. Each year I wondered, *Had he the money to pay?*

I didn't understand the hustle and bustle of the busy schedule and didn't want to wait to play with my new doll.

Then, way down the alphabetical list, our name would be called. I recall the first year the number was three after my second sibling was added, then four and six. When our name was called, the deacons would bring the correct number of sacks to our family.

Each of us children got one of the sacks with its predictable contents: an apple, an orange, a few walnuts, big pecans, hazelnuts, a peppermint stick and perhaps a pack of sweet-smelling chewing gum.

Receiving those paper sacks was a special event in my childhood. I never saw any of those nuts any other time than when they appeared in my Christmas sack, nor did I have a sack full of goodies any other time. I loved the sounds of all those sacks crackling and crushing as it echoed in the church every Christmas Eve. The smell of the goodies added to the anticipation.

After the program, we'd go to my paternal grandma's house. She lived alone, holding to her old German lifestyle in spite of changes in the community. My siblings and I were her youngest grandchildren so there weren't any cousins our age around. We celebrated Christmas around her tree in the bedroom of her small three-room house. The cedar tree sat on a table, perhaps two or three feet tall. My father would often cut her tree in the cow pasture at the same time he cut one for our family. On the tree hung the same decorations every year.

Among the shiny decorations were little tin candle holders with new white candles placed carefully on the outer branches. My grandmother would light the candles. In the small bedroom our family sat on the side of the bed around the tree to watch the candles burn. If a limb began to singe, the adults would put out the smothering branch without any big ado. The smell of the fresh burnt cedar added to the ritual.

After this quiet, sacred act of watching the candles burn, we'd go into the kitchen around Grandma's table. Grandma set the lamp on the table. She had fruitcake—a very simple, hard cake filled with nuts, raisins and a few dates. If my aunt supplied Grandma with a few pieces of candied fruit, she'd decorate the top of the cake with it.

Grandma also always had homemade white bread with a mound of fresh butter and homemade jelly. Sometimes there might be cream cookies with a little sprinkle of sugar on top. She'd fix coffee milk for us children. The smell of the coffee perking on the kerosene burner filled the house, adding to the festive spirit.

Later, if Grandma could spare the oil to burn the extra lamp, we'd go into the adjoining room and play the Victrola.

There was no focus on gift-giving, or a big eating event. If my grandmother gave us gifts, it was a new handkerchief or pair of socks. The event seemed more like a ritual, repeated each year in the same way.

That ritual celebration at Grandma's house was important to me. She moved slowly and confidently about her home as she hosted this event. I recall her telling stories about her own family whom she wouldn't see for the holidays. Those stories revealed to me her love for her own siblings.

Upon returning home, one of my parents stoked the fire and added a log to make sure there would be coals to start a fire the next morning. The only light was an oil lamp. Due to cost of oil, that lamp didn't burn any longer than necessary. We kids sometimes wanted to play with our new dolls, but we were rushed off, and quickly tucked into big feather beds for the night. If the weather was severe we always had a warm brick at our feet.

There wasn't time to play, but after I got older I tried to steal a few minutes anyway. I didn't understand the hustle and bustle of the busy schedule and didn't want to wait until after Christmas to play with my new doll. I sometimes cried because I had to wait.

On Christmas morning we hurried into our new dresses once more. The custom again was the same—a church service at midmorning. When there were six of us kids, we four oldest girls would squeeze into the backseat of our '39 Ford. With no elbow room, there was usually bickering about space.

A few years later, after the twins were born, they sat up front with my parents. In my early childhood, we would stop on the hill and pick up Grandma to ride to church. Strange … I don't remember how Grandma got to church once our family was so big she couldn't ride with us anymore.

After Christmas services, we hurried home to eat dinner. As I recall it was nothing big judged in worldly terms, but it was special to us—a meal of hen with bread dressing, or perhaps a small turkey. My parents carefully slaughtered the bird with the least market value. My mother baked it early in the morning in her little oven that sat on top of one of the kerosene burners. She'd leave it in the oven to stay warm while we were at church.

The custom of having bread dressing was later replaced by cornbread stuffing, a thing that would have been unthinkable in my early childhood. In those early years the simple meal included a canned vegetable put up the previous summer and a rice dish sprinkled with sugar and cinnamon for dessert.

After dinner, we went to our maternal grandma's house. Since I was the eldest grandchild in this large family, there were always lots of cousins around. We played mostly outdoors. Late in the afternoon we'd have the traditional German coffee and cake.

Some of my most cherished memories are of my grandpa. Sometimes he would get a far-away look in his eyes. He might tell a story. Once he told of the Christmas trees all covered with ice and snow. Then he'd break out in song, singing *O Christmas Tree* and *Silent Night* and other favorite German carols. Those snow-covered trees dated to his childhood in Germany. That would have been before he was 6 years old, in the 1880s.

When Grandpa sang, his voice rang out in a melody that was so sweet to my ears. His whole body seemed to sing. I could have listened to him sing endlessly. I loved those beautiful Christmas carols. Sometimes other family members complained about his singing. I was always glad when he didn't listen and kept on singing.

It may seem strange today to have Christmas with so little focus on food and gift-giving.

For me those early Christmases created a foundation in my life. The real value of Christmas was that sense of community with God as its head. ✶

Gifts of the Heart

For a long time I really envied my Grandma and Grandpa Tate. Each Christmas when we journeyed the three or four miles to their home I always found the last part of the gravel country lane leading down to the house lined with cars of children and grandchildren who had come to see them on the special day.

Grandma and Grandpa had 11 children who lived into adulthood; most of those children had large families of their own, and each made the pilgrimage at the Yuletide to the little four-room house to show their love and honor toward the patriarch and matriarch of the family.

Some of my cousins were already grown and had families of their own. By the time Grandma and Grandpa's children, grand-children, great-grandchildren and the "in-laws" were included, there must have been over a hundred people show up on Christmas. We tried to come in shifts to control the crowding, but several families—ours included—had no telephone, so invariably it seemed as though we kids had to stay outside in the frosty December air to make room in the house for the adults and the smallest children.

We were summoned inside only when it was time for us to give Grandma and Grandpa the Christmas presents we had bought or made them. There, in the warmth of the tiny living room, they were holding court for the day. They were surrounded by dozens and dozens of gifts from as many progeny. I was amazed and, as I said, a little envious of anyone who received so many gifts each year.

With a little gentle coaxing from Daddy, I shyly walked up with some little something for each of them. I had saved pennies throughout the year and I used several on my Grandma and Grandpa Tate's gifts.

After they pulled open the primitive wrapping and made sufficient *oohs* and *aahs*

over whatever trinket I had selected, Grandpa reached down into a basket, rummaged around in it for a few seconds and pulled out a thin package marked "Kenneth." It was usually a handkerchief—one, not a package of three. Then it was "Thank you," followed with a big bear hug from each of my grandparents and a muffled "I love you!" I moved back outside to make room for the next gift-bearer.

Years later I realized the silliness of my envy. Most of the gifts we grandchildren brought were useless to Grandma and Grandpa. Yet there was always something in that basket—despite lean years—that had my name on it. How they afforded even the simplest things I will never know.

But one thing I do know. Christmas at Grandma and Grandpa's house was filled with enough love that it made the hard times pale in its glow, at least for a few days. That is the most important lesson in giving—and receiving—gifts of the heart in those Good Old Days gone by. ✳

—*Ken Tate, Editor*

Uncle Fred's Package

By Wilma Moody

I knew Christmas was on its way when my brother Jerry began asking, "Mamma, did it come today?"

Beginning the last week in November, Jerry would rush home from school, slam the back door and shout the same question every day until the box arrived. The rest of us children would be at his heels, anxiously awaiting Mamma's answer.

I don't remember Mamma ever giving a straight "yes." She would always counter with, "You know it's too early to expect a package," or, "These are hard times. There might not be a package this year."

Such comments never fazed Jerry. He firmly believed the package would arrive. If it didn't come one day, it would be delivered the next day. He was sure Uncle Fred wouldn't let us down.

Uncle Fred was a salesman for the Arm & Hammer Baking Soda Company. He drove a nice car and wore fancy clothes. We thought he was rich. He always brought us miniature sample boxes of Arm & Hammer soda which we used to brush our teeth. Sometimes he brought candy. These small gifts were appreciated, but the arrival of his Christmas package was the highlight of the year.

Jerry had become an expert at reading Mamma's face. He would say, "Now, Mamma, you know it's not right to lie." Finally, the day would come when Mamma had to admit the package had arrived.

From that moment until Christmas, Mamma never had a minute's peace. Jerry was constantly snooping. When he could not find the Christmas box anywhere, he would insist that it was in the big locked trunk. Then we would badger Mamma to just let us look at the size and feel the weight of the package. At last Mamma would bring the box out of hiding and place it on the dining table so we could all get a look at it.

Next, we would plead for her to open the box and just let us see the shape of our individual gifts. But Mamma's years of experience had taught her not to allow such freedom until Christmas Eve. After breakfast on that day, the gifts would be placed under the tree. By the end of the day we had thoroughly examined not only our own presents but all the others as well.

We felt the gifts. We shook them. We smelled them. We even weighed them on the kitchen scales. We made a million guesses as to what they contained.

The arrival of Uncle Fred's Christmas package was the highlight of the year.

After supper on Christmas Eve, the long-awaited gifts were placed in our laps. When the moment at last arrived, Jerry was the last one to open his present. It seemed he wanted to savor the moment as long as possible.

Only once was I disappointed in my gift. One Christmas I received a small green leather purse. I eagerly unfastened the clasp, expecting to find the treasures usually contained in the purses I had examined, but this new purse was only stuffed with paper to retain its shape. I threw the purse down. Sobbing, I declared I did not want it.

Mamma finally determined the cause of my sorrow and hurriedly placed pennies, a comb, a small mirror and a handkerchief in the purse. She shook the purse close to my ear and I could not resist the urge to explore it. I was elated with the contents and carried the purse for many years.

Uncle Fred is gone now and so is my brother Jerry, but the joy and anticipation of Uncle Fred's package is one of my fondest childhood memories. ✳

Christmas 1932

By Molly Stewart

> **"Santa will be awfully busy this year," my mother said. "He has so many little boys and girls to look after. There isn't much money for him to spend either."**

ad I been older, I would have known better than to ask for the doll carriage that Christmas of 1932.

The strangling fingers of the Depression had already caught hold and were tightening without mercy. In our family of four girls and two boys, things were never easy. Of necessity, most of our Christmas gifts were mittens and mufflers and socks and sweaters fashioned from old woolen garments which had been raveled, washed and reknit by the creative hands of our mother.

I was the youngest of our brood, and when I was not in my first-grade classroom I spent most of the time with my father. It was difficult enough for an able-bodied man to find a job in those days, and it was not unusual to see both young and old riding the rails in search of work. My father was asthmatic, and I can still recall him, gasping for a breath that I feared might be his last, and the self-administered injections of adrenaline that carried him through those trying times.

It was Mother, though, who first realized my desire. I was sitting at the kitchen table, painstakingly blocking out the letters to Santa, when she advanced silently to stand behind me.

"How do you spell 'carriage'?" I called loudly, not knowing anyone was near.

"C-a-r-r-i-a-g-e, dear." Her soft voice startled me and caused me to turn.

She was a striking woman, my mother, but then I guess every 6-year-old feels that way about the woman in her life. She was tall and straight, with gentle brown eyes and thick auburn hair sprinkled with gray. Mother's dark beauty was marred only by the rough elastic bandages bound tightly around her legs to lend support while she nursed her endless 12-hour shift at the mental hospital.

Her hand touched my shoulder as she read the smudged letter before me. "I don't know, dear; Santa will be awfully busy this year. He has so many little boys and girls to look after. There isn't much money for him to spend either. Many fathers are out of work. Perhaps he will have to bring food to some little people."

I didn't answer; I just sat, confidently sealing the envelope. He'd bring it. I just knew he'd bring the carriage. After all, I had never asked Santa for anything like this before.

Mother helped me print the address—"Santa Claus, North Pole"—and I gave it to her to mail.

The days passed quickly as I fingered through the slick, gaudy pages of the mail-order catalog. What would my carriage be like? It needn't be as large as that one beside the Sleeping Beauty doll. My doll, Bridget, her bald head chipped and cracked, her left leg patched with adhesive tape, would not need a big carriage like that. A small one would be fine. Santa would know.

As the big day drew nearer, the light in the kitchen burned long into the night. When Mother's working day was over and we kids were in bed, she would pull out the old treadle sewing machine and begin her next shift. I'd hear my parents' voices muffled by the whir of the machine as I snuggled deeper under the covers with visions, not of sugarplums, but of doll carriages, dancing through my head.

The day before Christmas Mother was home and, with the help of my dad and the six of us, she decorated the front room. We never had a tree that I remember, but then neither did any of our neighbors. There were some faded red and green garlands strung from the corners of the room. Where they crisscrossed in the center above the dangling light cord, we hung a silver bell. It was all so beautiful, I thought, as I crouched near the potbellied heater to watch the proceedings. Would I ever be able to wait … wait until my doll carriage arrived?

My brothers teased me as I hung my neatly mended stocking along with theirs on a line Dad had put up behind the heater.

"You'll get a frozen fish in your sock, Fuzzy," they chanted. "Santa saw you snitch the cookies yesterday. You'll get a fish for sure!"

I didn't care. Let them tease. I knew Santa wouldn't forget me, even if he hadn't answered my letter. He was busy, wasn't he? All that work to do! He'd remember.

Finally Mother said it was bedtime and there

was no argument that night. I closed my eyes tightly and tried hard to go to sleep. From behind the closed door I could hear their laughter and the sounds of the radio. The precious battery was usually saved for the news and the odd special program. My parents knew that once that battery was dead, the voice behind the frayed brown panel would remain silent for a long time. There was no money to be spent on luxuries.

Just when I thought sleep would never come, I must have dozed off, because when I opened my eyes, dawn was sending its reflection off the fresh snow and into my bedroom window. In the double bed across the room, my sisters still slept.

Silently I swung my feet onto the cold floor and tiptoed into the living room. My brothers were asleep on the opened Toronto couch in the corner, and I tried to be very quiet.

Then I saw it. It stood, partially hidden by the heater, its blue paint bright in the early morning dusk. It was the most magnificent carriage I had ever seen. I ran toward it calling, "I knew! I knew!" caring no longer that my family slumbered.

When I reached to touch it, my joy knew no bounds. There, in the deep recess of its curved body, lay a doll more beautiful than I had ever imagined! It was dressed in high style with a small scarf and mittens sprouting like bright red blossoms from the dark mossy green of its rough tweed coat and beret. My happiness was complete.

It wasn't until years later that I thought about it and realized that neither the carriage nor the doll was new. It didn't matter then nor does it now.

The doll's wonderful wardrobe could only have been made by my mother. I recognized the scraps of material—the cotton dirndl from the tail of Mom's faded housedress, the tweed ensemble from goods left from a skirt she had made a neighbor, the red knitted scarf and mittens. The miniature wooden suitcase covered with wallpaper had been my dad's contribution.

I'll never know how they managed the doll and carriage. My sisters can't remember, and it's too late to ask Mother and Dad. But remembering that light, burning long into the weary nights, how I loved them for it! ✳

Bus Stop

By Henry Chequer, Jr.

At Christmastime I will go downtown and I will look in the window of a store by the bus stop to see if a koala has been placed among the Christmas decorations, as has been done each year—how many years has it been? And if the owner should notice me standing there, she will wave and smile, and I will smile, and remember— remember a moment when years ago I glimpsed the tidings of Christmas in a kindly act of giving and in the love on a child's face.

A woman had then stood at the bus stop, her face drawn and tired, and angry at the long and cold wait.

The Christmas decorations on the street poles swayed and rustled in the gusting wind. The sound of Christmas carols came from the nearby Salvation Army booth—*Break Forth, O Beauteous, Heavenly Light* and *Joy to the World*—and the passing children's faces were bright in anticipation of toys, good things to eat, and seeing Santa.

At the store window a small child stood transfixed, gazing at the bright toys, the games, and especially the little toy koala. Her nose was pressed against the glass, and she clapped her hands in pure and simple joy at the sight. Her mother stood apart, coaxing, repeating gently at small intervals, "Come, come now; we have to go home."

They wore the same cotton dress material, ill fitting, faded and pathetically thin against the cold. The child's sweater was threadbare, and the mother clasped a frayed shawl around her shoulders. "Come," she repeated. "Come now, we have to go home." But the child remained pressed to the window.

The woman by the bus stop turned and saw the child at the store window, and she saw the child's tiny fingers tracing on the glass as if reaching out to caress the little koala.

The woman looked up the street and saw the oncoming bus. "Well, at last," she muttered. She turned and again looked at the child. For a few moments she hesitated. She had waited a long time for the bus and it would be a long, cold wait for the next one.

She went into the store and shortly reappeared, holding the koala. She handed

There was such a look of joy and love on the child's face when she took the gift.

it to the child. Never was there such a look of joy and love on a child's face as when the child took the gift.

The woman went back to the bus stop, but the long-awaited bus had left. She looked back to the child holding her gift, so lovingly, so gently. The strain of weariness left her face. She smiled. "Oh, the heck," she said. "I'll walk. It's such a beautiful day."

At Christmastime I will again look in the window of the store by the bus stop, and remember—remember a moment of compassion and love. ✶

The Christmas Snoop

By R.G. Hobday

One of my best Christmases was almost a disaster. It was during the Great Depression—a time, I have since learned, when financial considerations often subdued dreams and wishes, not only of kids, but of grown-ups, too.

We were well into the Christmas shopping season and my two brothers and I knew it was important to drop subtle hints as to what we wanted for Christmas. And, of course, as Christmas approached, there was a lot of tactful—actually, sneaky—snooping to find out what was hidden where.

We knew it was important to drop subtle hints about gifts. And as Christmas approached, there was a lot of tactful—actually, sneaky—snooping to find out what was hidden where.

As a holdover from Santa Claus days, the tree continued to appear after we kids had gone to sleep on Christmas Eve. It must have been difficult for the folks, but it was also economical. Christmas trees were free after 11 p.m. when the vendors abandoned them.

One year my Christmas snooping almost ruined my Christmas. I had been asking for a BB gun for years and hoped finally to get one. But during my snooping, I came upon a present that could only be a guitar. A guitar had been my secret wish ever since I saw my first singing cowboy movie. I had no idea the folks knew about it, but I was a kid and parents were a wondrous breed apart. I could hardly wait!

Then, when Christmas finally arrived, there it was—the glorious package! But when I opened it—no guitar! The barrel end of a Red Ryder BB gun was stuck in a carton and the stock end had looked like the key end of a guitar! I had the gift I had wanted for years—but I was disappointed! To this day I still hope the folks didn't see how I felt.

Fortunately, I was soon having so much fun plinking at targets and things that I forgot all about guitars. Years later, when I finally did get one, I quickly discovered that my skills and aptitude were better suited to BB guns. ✶

Christmas From The Heart

By Judi Weber

The days before Christmas were filled beyond capacity with last-minute gifts to be purchased, parking places to find and then rushing into the store to thread my way through the crowds in a futile attempt to find "just the perfect gift."

Christmas carols merrily flowed from overhead speakers, with long lines at the cashier's counter and even longer lines to have the gifts

wrapped. My arms overflowed with the gaily wrapped gifts as I struggled to make my way to my car and then home. …

Home to address Christmas cards, an attempt to keep in touch with friends we no longer saw or seemed to find the time to visit. The house must be immaculate … no dustballs or cobwebs at Christmas. There were beautiful decorations to add just the right festive touch to our home and to brighten the gray December days.

Days were filled with endless lists, never-ending chores and a growing sense of emptiness, isolation and longing. I felt empty; I knew the real meaning of Christmas, but seemed unable to find it within myself.

My list of household duties almost completed, I had to water the flowers which were wintered in the basement. Armed with plastic jugs of water, I made my way from the gray December day down the stairs into the even darker basement. I barely noticed my summer plants, now protected from the cold Missouri winter.

I was tired, becoming more depressed, when in the back of the basement I saw a glimmer of color, a brilliant gleam of red among the dark basement shadows. Carefully

I rearranged the plants so that I might reach the flash of red which temporarily brightened my day. As I moved the plants aside I was suddenly reminded of a summer day long ago when…

"Would you like a start of that cactus?" Kathryn asked. I had been standing on the porch, absent-mindedly touching the leaves of the plant. Who thinks of Christmas in July? She gazed lovingly at the plant and after what seemed like a long time, she softly began to tell me her story—the story that transported me back to the turn of the century, to a small Ozark farm.

"I was the eighth of nine children. When my younger brother was a year old our father died, leaving his young immigrant wife alone to raise their large family. Leaving all family behind, both our parents had immigrated from Europe to this new country.

Her gift, a breath of spring, hidden away in the dark basement, had burst into joyous red blossoms, each joyfully heralding the true spirit of Christmas.

Exploring their new country, they decided to settle on a farm near Lamar, Mo. We had little money; my mother and brothers worked in the fields, tended milk cows, horses and a large garden.

"Christmas was always very special to my little brother Conrad and me. Our older brothers would search the snowy fields in search of the 'perfect' cedar tree, remembering Mama's requirements: 'It needs to be just so tall and not too big around.' The tree was cut, loaded into the old horse-drawn sled, over the snow-covered fields and home to our warm home with Mama waiting.

"My brother and I would eagerly look through the frost-covered windows, each wanting to be the first to herald the news of our arriving 'perfect' tree.

"The tree was carefully brought into the parlor; we knew this was special because the front parlor was for very special occasions. We decorated our tree with strings of popcorn and cranberries, and bits of tinfoil fashioned into stars and tiny candles. Our oldest brother would light each candle and the sight was a glory to behold.

"Then Mama would disappear, down into the cellar. When she returned, her arms held the beautiful shimmering Christmas cactus, all covered with cascades of flaming red blossoms. Mama's Christmas cactus had spent the fall sitting quietly in our cellar. Gifts were a luxury

strayed to the quilt-covered basket Mama had placed under the tree. Mama went to the tree and carefully reached down into the basket.

"As she stood up, her hands held a large flaming Christmas cactus. 'I wanted you to have your own plant, so after you married I took a start from my own cactus,' she softly said, with tears in her eyes.

"Mama had cared for and nurtured the small plant and, with her care, it had grown into the beautiful plant she now held in her hands. Holidays came and went, Mama passed away, my brothers married and moved away, but her gift continued to bloom and brighten each and every Christmas."

Sitting on the shelf at the back of the basement, I saw Kathryn's gift to me— the beautiful red plant with its long leaves ablaze with bright red blossoms.

Her gift, a breath of spring, hidden away in the dark basement, had burst into joyous red blossoms, each joyfully heralding the true spirit of Christmas.

The plant's simple gift of love, giving of itself, bespoke the true meaning of Christmas. My fatigue faded; I forgot about the meaningless lists and chores. Christmas gifts come from hearts and hands, not from stores and checkbooks. Gifts of love must be tenderly created and nurtured by hands and heart.

Kathryn's gift of love—her mother's gift—will always be cherished. With love and nurturing, new plants will grow into "just the perfect gift"—gifts from the heart—to be cherished and passed on to brighten other homes and other hearts. ✳

we could not afford but the Christmas cactus was a luxury for our hearts and our eyes.

"Years later my husband and I started our own home. Our first Christmas would be lonely until Mama's letter announced that she and my brothers would pay a Christmas visit.

"The frosty morn arrived; the old Model T pulled up in front of our house and Mama and my brothers jovially piled from the car. Mama's arms contained a large quilt-covered basket. As they shook the snow from their coats, their laughter and presence soon filled our home with joy. Gifts were a luxury we could not afford, so we exchanged simple, love-made gifts, gifts from the heart.

"As we began to open our gifts, my eyes

Grandma's Christmas

By Letha Fuller

All the family wondered,
What would please dear Grandma most
For a Christmas present?
"I have everything," she'd boast.

Grandma was very practical.
Fancy gifts were not her way.
Unless 'twas something she could use
She was sure to give it away.

This was a special Christmas …
Grandma was 83.
We all asked her what she'd like,
But all five asked secretly.

"A nice warm woolly nightgown
Would suit me to a T.
That's all I want for Christmas!"
She told each one emphatically.

Christmas morn arrived
With many gifts beneath the tree.
Everyone was opening them
Excited as could be!

Old Santa placed by Grandma's chair
Five boxes gayly wrapped.
Her big brown eyes sparkled
And her wrinkled hands clapped.

She untied the ribbons,
Opened a box with care.
"A beautiful pink nightgown—
Just what I need to wear!"

We watched her open packages
Quite alike in size.
Each contained a lovely nightie
Much to her surprise!

Tears glistened as she exclaimed,
"What a Christmas! Sakes alive!
I really needed a nightie
But did you have to buy me five?" ✳

We soon learned if we turned the big package a certain way it uttered a faint "Ma-ma" sound. We had never heard such a thing!

The Mystery Package

By June Morris

The memory of the Christmas of 1923 is still vivid in my mind 71 years later.

We were a young family of eight consisting of six siblings, Mommy and Daddy. We lived in the tiny village of Blaine, Kan., where we had just moved from Sedalia, Mo., because of the infamous railroad strike of 1922.

The strike was called because the Missouri Pacific Railroad Company had cut the men's wages 5–7 percent by July 4 due to the fact the end of World War I cut demands. It was never settled, so the people had to either go back to farms or leave town to find other jobs.

We moved by train to Blaine so Daddy could work at the Sinclaire Pipeline Pumping station. We needed a lot of things that we had to leave in Sedalia. Mommy and Daddy immediately sent off for a Montgomery Ward catalog. Our baby brother was born soon after the move, and, as well as I can remember, there was no place in town to buy baby and household needs. The catalog was very important to furnish these necessities.

This little village had a town pump in the center of the T-shaped intersection of the main dirt street. We little girls thought it was a novelty to pump a drink into the tin can that hung on the pump. I also remember there were only a combined grocery store-post office, a small hotel and a tiny yellow shed-like train depot in town.

We lived in the last house on this road in town, and it was we children's daily chore to walk down to the post office to collect our mail when we got home from school. We looked forward to this great adventure each day because we sometimes received a package from Montgomery Ward's.

One day that winter there was a large package wrapped in heavy brown paper and securely tied with a small rope. There was some discussion about us taking it home. They decided to let us take it after we assured them that we three little girls, 8, 7 and 5, could carry it home. Little did we know how heavy it was! As we struggled we soon learned we could not carry it in our tiny arms; we had to carry it by the rope.

Of course, we had to set it down many times to rest and relax our arms. We also turned it every way possible to find an easier way to carry it—but to no avail. We soon learned if we turned the big package a certain way it uttered a faint "Ma-ma" sound. We had never heard such a thing. We became so curious about what caused that strange sound that we hurried home as fast as possible. We were anxious to get home and have Mommy open it to see what was in that package. But Mommy had other plans.

She explained the package was for Santa and not us. We firmly believed anything Mommy said and were perfectly willing to do anything Santa Claus desired. We were satisfied not to open the box.

We carried it into the bedroom, and Mommy climbed on top of the old white treadle sewing machine and struggled until she pushed the box up into the attic to save for Christmas Eve when Santa could stop and pick it up to deliver to some good boys and girls as he rode his sleigh that night.

When Christmas morning came, we woke up when we heard Daddy building a fire in the heating stove. But Mommy made us stay in bed until the room warmed up.

When we got up there was a 27-inch red metal wagon with a big doll sitting in it that said "Ma-ma"—just like that strange sound we'd heard in the mystery package. There was also a large bag of Christmas candy and one of nuts, a large red rubber ball, a can of Prince Albert tobacco and three china bowls under the Christmas tree.

It took me several years to figure out that mystery package. ✶

The "Topsy-Turvy" Christmas

By Doreen LaChambre Houston

As it is with most preschool children, I had no sense of years. Days, however, I understood well, and I anxiously marked each number on the December page of our calendar as I waited for Christmas. The year probably read 1931 or 1932.

It was a time when my parents often used the word "Depression."

With my two older sisters now in school, I delighted in my private relationship with Mama. The wind howled on that special afternoon when Mama and I ventured out to do some shopping. Down Higgins Avenue we struggled against the storm until we reached Woolworth's Five-and-Dime store. There in the window I saw her, the most beautiful doll in the world!

Peering through the slit between the cap pulled down over my forehead and the scarf tied around my face, my eyes caressed her. She had short brown hair like mine and sleep eyes, and wore a white dress and bonnet trimmed with pink ribbons. I wanted that doll and knew just how to get her. I would send my plea to Santa Claus and promise a life of such angelic goodness that he couldn't refuse me.

> *I wanted that doll and knew just how to get her. I would send my plea to Santa Claus and promise a life of such angelic goodness that he couldn't refuse me.*

That afternoon I anxiously waited for my sister Elaine to return from school. "Please help me write a letter," I begged. Carefully I copied the words she put on a paper for me. I reaffirmed my promise of saintly behavior, and described the doll.

"You will find her in the window at Woolworth's store," I told Santa, just in case he didn't have one like her at the North Pole. Mama knew how much I wanted that doll and warned several times, "Other little girls want that doll too, and perhaps some other child might need her more." But my faith was strong. I knew!

The day finally came when I marked the number 24 on our calendar. For weeks I had been uncommonly good, and I could almost feel a shiny halo around my head. Christmas Eve our family gathered in the kitchen while Daddy removed pits from dates, and replaced them with walnuts. Then we three girls rolled the fruit in sugar. Sugar-dates were Daddy's favorite holiday treats, and helping prepare them was a Christmas Eve tradition for my sisters and me.

The soft falling snow had blanketed our world in a white coverlet. With our dates finished, Daddy went out to shovel the walks, and his three girls followed him into the crisp night. While Daddy dug a gorge through the drifts, we happily played at creating snow angels by falling back into the fresh snow and frantically moving our arms and legs up and down. By the time Daddy finished his snow removal we girls had filled the yard with angel impressions we hoped would please the little Baby Jesus.

Mama had put sugar-water on the stove to boil while we were outside. "Bring me the big mixing bowl," Daddy called through the kitchen door. Then he scooped a cloud of clean snow into the bowl, and we all trooped into the warmth of the kitchen. Slowly Daddy poured the cooked sugar-water back and forth into the snow-filled bowl, weaving thin lines of hot liquid that quickly turned into sweet candy. It was grand! We sat in the glow of our lighted tree, picking sweet bits of candy from the bowl. All too soon the clock chimed, signaling our bedtime.

I tossed fretfully in bed, squirming and kicking my annoyed sister. Under the pretext of needing the bathroom I got up. In the kitchen Mama was mixing bread stuffing for Christmas dinner. Daddy sat at the table carefully cutting and trimming pieces of heavy cardboard to fit inside his little girls' worn-out shoes. He performed this feat often and could make fine, smooth insoles that would keep the cold dampness from our feet for quite

The falling snow had blanketed our world in a white coverlet. Daddy went out to shovel the walks, and his three girls followed him into the crisp night.

a while, although sometimes the shoes would be a little tight for a few days after their reconstruction.

It was a night of excitement, and I ran to hug my parents again before I was returned to bed by Mama, who seemed strangely melancholy as she kissed me goodnight.

Finally, the seemingly endless night gave way to a pearly haze showing under the window

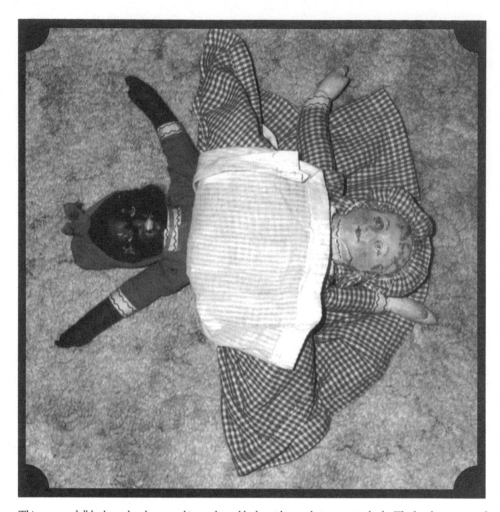

heads, one white and one black, with yarn hair covering both. The heads were joined at the waist, and a long skirt covered either head so that the "topsy-turvy" thing could make two separate dolls.

My heart thumped with shivery jerks. Something in the air felt heavy and hurtful, as if a polluted fog filled the room. Deep inside me an unfamiliar stirring began, perhaps giving birth to my first act of compassion. Trying to understand the sadness on Mama's face, I took the rag doll from her hugged it. *Well, it's OK,* I thought.

After all, I had candy in my stocking, a coloring book and new games that I knew Daddy would play with us after breakfast. It would be a merry Christmas. I smiled at Mama, who smiled back with a

This strange doll had two heads, one white and one black, with yarn hair covering both. The heads were joined at the waist, and a long skirt covered either head so that the "topsy-turvy" thing could make two separate dolls.

shade. "Is it time? Can we get up?" I called out. Our sleepy father went down to light the tree, and we girls dashed after him. When the bright lights flicked on my eyes swept the room, searching for her. "Where is she? Where?" I couldn't see my doll. Puzzled and uncertain I froze in the moment, not knowing what to do. Maybe Santa didn't get my letter!

Mama picked up something under the tree and held it out to me. "See, Honey, I think Santa left this for you." Stunned disbelief seemed to separate me from my body. As if fastened to the floor, Mama stood rigid and unmoving holding that cloth doll.

This was a mistake! I felt my chin wiggling in disappointment. I had seen a doll like that at the house of Mama's friend who sometimes sewed toys. Why would Santa get a doll from Mrs. Weinrich? The strange rag doll had two

look of sweet relief in her eyes. The dreadful unknown in the room seemed to leak away.

I don't remember naming my rag doll. I didn't like her very much, but I mothered her as best I could, trying not to show my true feelings. Somehow I realized the need to conquer my disappointment and accept the gift.

Over the years Santa brought me other dolls. I loved them all, but the "topsy-turvy" ragsy thing is one I remember well. I often recall that bittersweet Christmas.

Even now the memory rekindles an ache in my heart for my worried parents, and I feel again the confusion, disappointment and final acceptance of a little girl. Perhaps that Christmas was my rite of passage, for with childlike innocence it was then that I offered my first true gift to another—one of love and compassion for my anxious parents. ✳

A Basket Full of Christmas

By Rae Cross

Today, as I browsed through a Goodwill store, I saw a big wicker clothes basket. Memories of "Christmas Past" rushed in.

I didn't realize how long I had stared at the basket until a clerk asked if she might help. When I said, "No thank-you, I was just thinking about Christmas," she gave me an odd look and, I feel certain, passed the word that I should be watched. Thinking about it later, I can understand her concern, because Christmas and clothes baskets don't seem to have much in common. However, at our house years ago, the two were almost synonymous.

Immediately after Thanksgiving dinner, we all began urging Mother, "Now can we put the basket out?"

Reluctantly, she always agreed—reluctantly, because the only place where it could be placed was on top of the huge grand piano which dominated the living room with its bulk and massive legs. It was Mother's prize possession, and nothing, but nothing, was placed on its polished top until it was carefully padded and protected from scratch or stain. Finally pronounced ready, the oversized basket, with red bows tied on each handle, was placed on top of the blankets and coverings and "Christmas began."

Even if we could have afforded a tree, the room could not have accommodated both the tree and the piano. Certainly a tree could not have brought more happiness or excitement than the clothes basket. As days went by, packages were placed in

Certainly a tree could not have brought more happiness or excitement than the clothes basket. As days went by, packages were placed in it, and with each one, our suspense increased.

it, and with each one, our suspense increased.

We knew most presents would, of necessity, be useful—clothes, mittens, boots, caps, earmuffs and scarves. Knowing that did not dampen our impatience or anticipation for, in addition to the expected gifts, we each gave to other family members a "fun gift." This gift was not to cost more than 10 cents, but it was amazing what you could buy at the dime store those days, and oh, the thrill of shopping! These little gifts were wrapped so no one could guess what the package contained. Little packages, big packages and middle-size ones were all wrapped in tissue paper and decorated with pictures cut from magazines and papers.

When at last the wonderful day finally came and my father lifted the overflowing basket onto the floor, we all gathered 'round, and since I was the youngest, I generally was privileged to call out the names and deliver the gifts!

We never knew whether a package would contain a warm sweater, long johns, or one of the various fun items, such as a pencil (maybe an advertising one from a local store; so what? It would write), a shoe horn, a thimble, a jackknife, shoestrings, tape measure, eraser,

package of needles, handkerchief, hair ribbons, buttonhook, dust cap, pocket comb, candy bar, jacks or whistle. Each gift brought shouts of joy and unaffected pleasure.

When the bottom of the basket was reached, Mother always said, "Now we can put all the dirty clothes in the basket and clear off the top of the piano."

Somehow we knew that meant she wanted to be asked to play the Christmas hymns we knew so well. Never did a happier group gather around and sing with all the ardor of the true Christmas spirit and our family relationship.

The empty basket at the Goodwill store was reminiscent of the emptiness I know now at this season when it is no longer possible to enjoy the love and companionship of those happy days, and yet I envision the basket—full, and running over—with gratitude for the love and blessings the years gave and have brought so generously to me and mine.

And how I hope that everyone, everywhere, may have a Christmas basket—real and mental—full of life's necessities and enough fun to lighten life's seriousness, and always a song to summarize the meaning and the glory of the day. ✶

The 10-Cent Christmas

By Jeannette Clark

It was 1931, in the depth of the Depression. My mother, father, five of my six brothers and I were living in the drafty old colonial house we had moved into a few years before and which we had been in the process of renovating ever since. My sixth and oldest brother, John, lived far away in the north of the state, suffering with his wife and six young children through a bitter winter of unemployment, cold and deprivation.

We were luckier than some families in our town. My father, a traveling salesman, continued to draw a regular salary, even though the commissions on his sales of food colors and extracts had dropped to nearly zero. He still went out on his business trips each week, but in January and February he would be staying at home. There was simply not enough business in the middle of winter to make it profitable for the company to pay his travel expenses.

> *That Christmas, only one of my brothers was working. Andy brought home the paltry sum of $20 for a 72-hour week at the local drugstore.*

Only one of my brothers was working. Andy brought home the paltry sum of $20 for a 72-hour week at the local drugstore, and $8 of that went to Mother for board. His tedious job had one advantage: he could buy at a discount the cigarettes and razor blades that he doled out to Joe and Tom, who had been unemployed for months. Whenever he could, he slipped each of them a dollar or two so that they wouldn't have to ask Mother for spending money.

Joe had come home in the fall from his job on the government dredge in the Sacramento River. He had left home two years before and joined the hordes of boys and girls who journeyed west in search of some kind of work, thumbing their way, "riding the rails" or walking long, weary miles. They slept in the open or in empty freight cars until chased away by railroad police. They warmed themselves at campfires and ate out of tin cans in the company of hoboes of all ages and descriptions. Even though Joe had found work easily and was making good money, he gave it all up to cross the country to be with the family again. He didn't want to spend another Christmas away from home.

Joe was not too proud to put his name on the town list for shoveling whenever there was a snowstorm big enough to warrant adding to the regular highway crew, but Tom, who had lost his job on a Boston newspaper when everything went down the drain, could not bear to become a public spectacle. Every week or so, he pressed his only suit, polished his shoes, and set out to make the rounds of businesses in town, hoping to find a vacancy created since his previous visit. He waited anxiously each day for the mail, hoping for an answer to one of his many job applications.

Three of us were still young enough to be in school. I suppose we really had little idea of the meaning of the Depression, since our days passed in routine fashion. We heard stories, of course, of schoolmates who had to stay home because they had no warm clothes. It was even rumored that one family lived for a whole week on a bushel of apples.

We knew that children who lived close to the railroad tracks found a way to get through the fence around the coal pile and picked up enough coal after dark to keep their kitchen fires going. When our own supply of coal ran low, we would keep the furnace fire going with discarded wooden heels from the shoe factory or untrimmed slabs of wood from the lumber yard. To conserve heat, we lived mostly in the kitchen and sitting room with the rest of the house shut off. At night, the bedroom doors were opened briefly to take the deathly chill from the rooms before we slithered into our clammy beds.

My mother often had to dig down deep into her worn handbag for the money we deposited each week in the school bank. She treated every coin as if it were a fortune, and saved in every way possible. She ladled steaming soups and stews into our bowls and filled us up with cooked cereals, eggs and homemade bread. She was not above buying clothes at rummage sales, and she skillfully mended and darned hand-me-downs.

It must have been a mild December evening that I remember, for we were gathered around the Franklin stove in the long living room that we seldom used in winter. Father was away, as usual, on a business trip. Mother came from the kitchen, drew some dog-eared bills from her apron pocket, and spoke with her customary firmness.

"I've thought it all over and decided to give each of you a dollar to spend on presents this year. It's all I can spare and it will make all of us equal in giving. We're going to have a 10-cent Christmas. Ten cents may not seem like much, I know, but I expect you to put on your thinking caps and make it a good time for everyone."

There never was a Christmas when we were closer to each other.

and warm cast-off clothing. We could just picture the expressman lugging the box up their front steps and their children running to open the door in their only excitement of the Christmas season.

I have no clear memory of the contents of the packages that peeped out from the branches of the tree Joe and Tom had brought in from the woods. There must have been a bottle of cheap cologne, some handkerchiefs and peppermint drops for Mother. No doubt Father got one or two of his favorite 7–20–4 cigars, and perhaps even a rayon polka-dot bow tie. We younger children must have exchanged pen holders and nibs as well as miniature toys. Probably there were enough packages of Lucky Strikes (10 cents at that time) to keep the older boys in luxurious clouds of smoke for a week or two.

There were some unforgettable gifts. Joe, who was always resourceful, used his money to buy scraps of leather and wood to make a variety of ornaments and jokes for each member of the family.

He rewarded Andy's patience and generosity with a leather medal to hang by a blue ribbon around his neck. He carved a wooden horse for the youngest brother, who had a passionate love for anything on four feet.

A 10-cent Christmas! We had hardly thought about what we would get or give for presents. Last Christmas had been lean enough, with only a few packages under our tree, and this year promised to be even more meager. But only a dime to spend for each one! How could we possibly do it?

It was lucky that Woolworth's really was a "five-and-ten" in those days. Nickels and dimes could go a long way; in fact there was almost too much to choose from. I remember hurrying downtown after school to hang over the counter for an hour or more selecting gifts. If one of my brothers happened to come in on the same errand, we carefully hid our purchases.

Part of each dollar went for a toy to go into John's box for his children. Mother packed a huge carton with our small gifts, canned goods,

I remember perspiring over a wallpaper-covered notebook for Mother to keep her recipes in, and fastening pieces of felt together for a pen wiper for Father. Mother knitted her usual heavy, scratchy mittens from raveled-out sweaters, and Father presented each of us with a small leather-bound diary (a free annual gift to his company's customers) that gave us a sense of importance even though we had few "engagements" to write in it.

There never was a Christmas when we were closer to each other. I can still feel the ache in my jaws from laughter over each gift, whether funny or practical. Mother had given us a dollar to spend, and with it, a fortune in togetherness. It may have been, as Dickens put it, the worst of times, but for us, our 10-cent Depression Christmas was the best we ever had. ✶

Our Best Christmas Memory

By Mrs. Merl Park

Our five children, two girls and three boys, are all grown up now, but that Christmas was the best one we ever had.

It was in the early '40s during World War II. My husband and I decided we would make the toys for our children's Christmas.

We started early in October on them. Our oldest boy and girl were to help us make them. The boy was about 12 and the girl, 10. Of course, we had to wait until the three little ones were in bed and asleep before we could begin work. Then we would keep at it until 1 or 2 a.m.

We made stuffed animals—horses and dogs—and built trains for the boys. To make these trains we used wooden cheese boxes, the long, narrow kind, for the boxcars. We made the engines out of 1-by-4 strips with a 2-by-4 whittled out to make the boiler and cab and nailed onto the 1-by-4.

The wheels we made out of lathes which we cut out square and then whittled round, by hand.

The smokestacks were made out of empty thread spools. We painted the engine black and then trimmed it in red. The cars we painted different colors.

We built the children each a barn out of hard boards and painted them red with green roofs.

My husband and I built a barn and train for the oldest boy and a cedar chest for the girl which we painted walnut color. It was pretty and she

loved it very much. (She still has it and still likes it.)

In order for these to be a surprise we had to work on them after the older ones had gone to bed, after we had finished all of the younger children's toys.

I made rag dolls, quilts, pillows, sheets and blankets for the girls, and we also made them each a cute little doll cradle and painted them a pretty blue.

A few days before Christmas, we took the family and drove up to the mountains and cut a pretty cedar tree. It was very beautiful and had its natural berries of blue-gray still on its branches. It filled the house with its fragrant odor.

We made many of our trimmings out of egg shells which we painted different colors. We put glue on some and sprinkled glitter on them. We glued a loop of string to each so we could hang them on the branches.

I will never forget the picture that Christmas morning—the pretty tree, which filled the corner of our living room, with its homemade trimmings, and the bright, colorful array of toys under it. The tree and toys extended out almost into the center of the room.

Our children were very happy with the toys and the tree. The toys cost a very small amount of money. We were happy to have been able to make them. There was satisfaction in our accomplishment. The one regret was that we did not take any pictures.✶

Chapter Four

Lights of the Season

 When electricity finally made it to our little neck of the woods, the changes were immediate and profound (at least they seemed profound to us). Of course the most profound change was that of lighting the old home place. Daddy ran wires around the attic and put a single porcelain fixture in the middle of each of our three rooms.

There was no light switch; it took a lot less wiring to have a pull-chain for each of the lights. It was magic to pull that string and have the room flooded with incandescence.

There were no wall outlets. That also would have meant pulling walls down to run wiring, and Daddy wasn't too sure this newfound, newfangled "convenience" would be worth all of that work. We were able to plug the few things that needed to be plugged into a single outlet in the light fixture. Besides lights, there weren't that many changes in our lives those first couple of years.

But when Christmas that first year rolled around—now, *that* was special! To that point we had decorated trees the old-fashioned way, with strings of popcorn, a few small ornaments and stars we three kids had cut in school and brought home to surprise Mama and Daddy.

And then there was light! It impressed me as much as if it had been the first light of Creation. And now, in the Christmas season, Daddy brought home something even more impressive—a short strand of electric Christmas lights. We sang carols as we ceremoniously draped the wires around the tree. No more would we have a drab, darkened tree, lit only by the kerosene lantern. Now our front room window would gleam with the lights of the season!

The second or third time we plugged in those lights we had a rude awakening. There was a pop and the bulbs which had so brilliantly lit the tree one moment just as quickly went dark.

Many of you will remember when one burnt-out bulb meant a break in the circuit, followed by darkness. Daddy had prepared for just such an "emergency" (it seemed big to us children), and had brought a couple of extra bulbs home as well. Now the only problem was the needle-in-a-haystack search for the one bulb which was the culprit. Later I wondered what we would have done if two bulbs had simultaneously gone out.

That first year, when Daddy wasn't sure if this new electrifying experience might burn down our little home, he didn't let us leave the tree lights on all of Christmas Eve. I guess Santa must have plugged them into that porcelain light fixture. Bright and early Christmas morning, when we piled into the still-cold, still-dark living room, the tree glowed with the colors of the season. It was still a fairly meager Yuletide, but for the first time we saw the hopeful lights of the season in the Good Old Days.

—Ken Tate, Editor

A Story Told By Christmas Ornaments

By Gloria Bundy

$\mathcal{I}$t's Epiphany, Jan. 6, the day that traditionally the wise men came to the stable to see the Christ-child. Now, Christmas is over! It's time to take down the decorations, store them for next year and go on with our lives.

As I took the ornaments off the tree I was reminded of family members not with us anymore—of Christmases past. Many ornaments have memories associated with them, and have been on our Christmas trees for generations.

I took the solid blue ornament off and held it to look at its workmanship again, as I do every Christmas. It is one Grandpa brought with his belongings when he came to live with our family after Grandma died in 1941. It is solid, not hollow like many modern ornaments, and the manger is embedded in the mold of the ornament.

A solid ornament, meant to last, I thought. *It reminds me of Grandpa, a solid, sturdy German who always built and worked to make everything of lasting value.* The ornament hung on the trees in his boyhood home on the farm in the 1860s and 1870s.

When I was a child Dad had a country store and the day after Thanksgiving he and Mom displayed the Christmas merchandise. An old man from a nearby farm came each year and brought a cedar tree which they decorated after the store was closed, at 7 o'clock. Among the displays for sale were Christmas tree ornaments. Among the ornaments I took off my tree this year were ornaments from Dad's store.

I thought of how carefully Dad and Mom handled them when a purchase was made. Dad would wrap each in a piece of newspaper, then carefully put them into a box. They weren't solid, but were made of thin glasslike material that broke easily.

I held the doll ornament for a moment when I took it off the tree. I thought of how I, as a child, always admired it on Aunt Leona's tree. One year she took it off her tree and gave it to me.

Dad would hand the box to the purchaser and say, "They are 5 cents apiece. That would be 30 cents for all of them."

Time passed and World War II was upon us. No longer were the beautifully colored ornaments available; now they were plastic. We purchased a few new ones and I took down a little red boot, a little red house and a little red bell. Dad no longer had the store and helped with decorating our tree at home.

Mom, Grandpa and I all shared in the joy of putting up the tree, but something was not right. We thought of so many of "our boys" fighting in foreign lands, languishing in prison camps and sent home because of injuries. My own husband was in far-off Okinawa.

Finally the war was over and my husband came home. During the Korean War we settled into our home on the farm where Grandpa grew up. A few days before Christmas we walked out into the woods and cut our own little cedar tree. We put it into a stand and set it in our living room, then went shopping for ornaments.

This year brought another milestone in ornaments: About all that was available were plastic foam ones. They had different shapes—bells, snowballs and stars, among others—and all were white. *A far cry,* I thought, *from the colorful ones Dad once sold in his store*. But we bought enough for our little tree, and after we hung them and strung the electric lights we thought it looked pretty—after all, it was our first tree together. When I took these ornaments off my tree this year, I noticed that they were all there; not much can happen to a plastic foam ornament!

I held the ones our oldest son created with Mom, when he was little. They used some of our plastic foam ones and decorated them with Christmas seals and ribbons. My thoughts went back more than 40 years when he and Mom created all kinds of things for the Christmas season, including a paper chain made of construction paper.

As I took down what remains after all these years I carefully folded it and put it in a bag; maybe it can hang on the tree just one more year.

I held the doll for a moment when I took it off the tree. I thought of how I, as a child,

always admired it on Aunt Leona's tree. One year she took it off her tree and gave it to me. It wore a skirt of tiny feathers. I thought it was a real treasure. Long ago the feathers began to fall off, but the doll hangs on my tree every year.

I took down the celluloid doll that my grandma and grandpa had on their tree before 1941. Grandma dressed it in a tiny dress and didn't forget to also sew a pair of tiny, blousy bloomers to match the dress.

Today craft shops are flourishing and ladies are making ornaments out of felt decorated with sequined designs, and crocheted covers over shiny, colored balls. I recently bought a few and received some as gifts from friends.

This year before Christmas I was elated to find a gift shop with a Christmas tree with ornaments molded exactly like the ones Dad sold in the days of my childhood. They were made in Germany and no longer cost "5 cents apiece." Nevertheless, I bought four of them.

I especially wanted the colorful bird with the white plastic tail, which clips on a branch. Dad, who disliked change so much, would be smiling to see the bird perched on my tree which his great-granddaughter Catherine and I cut down in the woods out behind the barn. ✶

A Tree—No Matter How

By Betty Piazzi

When I was a child many years ago, my two sisters and I were left in the care of our grandparents for several years. They were a wonderful couple, and tried to teach us right from wrong, and especially to be truthful. We were old enough to know that there wasn't much money for Christmas, but young enough to wish and hope for things. The one thing we felt we had to have was a Christmas tree; it just wouldn't be Christmas without a tree.

We giggled and planned after we were in bed, like all little girls over the world—and oh, how the time dragged. Finally, Grandma said we'd really start planning for Christmas now. So we went all over the fields to hunt hickory nuts and walnuts for cookies and cakes—also to find any kind of red berries and leaves to decorate our tree. One trip when Grandma went with us, we gathered pokeberries in a bucket, and she peeled the bark from a certain kind of tree and carried it home in her apron. She cooked the bark and it made a bright orange-colored water, and of course, the pokeberries made a blood-red water. Grandma put back a bucket of each color to dye a quilt lining (made from white flour sacks) and maybe a few of our faded and worn dresses. We also made a pan of strong bluing water.

As the time grew nearer, we popped big pans of popcorn. I can just see the four of us, sitting around that pan stringing the fluffy white corn on long strings that had no end.

Next, we heated the "dye water" and dipped the long strings in them, coming out with red, orange and blue decorations for the tree. Then Grandma sent us out to pick all the little pieces of wool that hung on the barbed-wire fences from the sheep scratching on the fence, or maybe trying to get under the fence. She dipped them in alum water (at least I think it was alum water), and they sparkled like they had silver dust on them when we tied them on the tree.

Well, we had all the decorations for the tree—but still had no tree, and no kind of cedar or evergreen grew on our grandparents' farm. We knew there were some on another farm close by though, and we decided we'd go get one. They were probably gone to the city, and after all, they wouldn't miss just one! We took along an old hatchet, and just as we got the tree chopped down, a hunter fired a gun at a rabbit, and the bullet went singing right close to us. We started to run, dragging the tree as we went, and never looked back until we got home. Of course, we had to explain where we got the tree. Grandpa said, "For shame! You go get a tree without asking, when Mr. Trent told me we were welcome to have one for our Christmas."

Our punishment was to say "Christmas tree" over and over 100 times. We decorated the tree, and it did look pretty, but as Grandpa said, it would have been much prettier if we had asked our neighbor for the tree. My littlest sister said, "Well, we had to have it for Jesus' Birthday!" ✳

Secondhand Tree

By Gertrude Albert

*I*t happened on Dec. 24, 1930. Our house was filled with the spicy aroma of the sauerbraten Mama was simmering in the kitchen. Brother Fritz was practicing his violin in the bedroom with the door closed. I was in the dining room reading *The Bobbsey Twins* and Papa's workday ended an hour early so he went to "the avenue" to pick out a Christmas tree.

We had no car, so Mama couldn't get the Christmas tree. She did all she could do just to lug groceries home across the open prairie.

She said, "Gertie, look out and see if Papa is coming. I can't start my potato dumplings until he is in sight."

> **Papa said, "Fritz, get your violin and I will light our candle in remembrance of Jesus who brought light to the world."**

Hopping up, I licked my thumb good before placing it on the frosted window. A peephole just large enough to peer through appeared. The dried grass was covered with snow, which the restless wind had sculpted into intriguing swirls. Zeroing in on the shortcut path, I saw a figure approaching.

Giving the peephole another thumb treatment, I looked again.

"Mama, Papa is coming but he doesn't have a Christmas tree, just a small paper bag."

The violin squeaks stopped and Fritz came running to the window. He scratched off some frost, peeked out and said, "She's right, Ma, no tree."

Together we bolted to the kitchen where Mama was lowering the dumplings into the boiling pot. Before we could say a word she cautioned, "Don't pester your father the minute he comes in. He is probably half frozen after that long walk. Wait to hear what has happened."

Fritz and I exchanged glances before returning to our separate activities.

The book no longer interested me. All I could think of were the ornaments on the shelf in the closet. Without a tree we couldn't take turns hanging them. Nor would Mama be able to explain, "This one is a zeppelin from Germany," or, "The glass gypsy was made in Czechoslovakia."

Then I heard Papa stomping up the back stairs and I almost beat Fritz to the kitchen. When the door opened we said, "Hello Papa."

"Hello kids, hello Pauline. I walked the full length of the avenue without finding a Christmas tree. The grocers said they bought too few. Since the stock market crash business is slow and they were afraid that the trees wouldn't sell. Never mind. This year we will have a Christmas table. Look!"

Papa opened the brown bag and pulled out a big red candle. "We will light this in remembrance of Jesus who came to the earth so long ago."

Disappointed that we wouldn't have a tree, tears filled my eyes and a few splashed out. Of course, Fritz noticed and poked me, whispering, "Don't be a baby."

Papa must have known we felt sad because after he put his overshoes on the newspaper beside the door he turned to us and said, "Fritz, Gertie, even if we have no tree, Mama has a fine dinner and afterwards we will have a family Christmas Eve celebration."

"All right, Papa," we chimed halfheartedly.

After dinner Mama laid her best cloth on the dining room table and put the red candle right in the center. She got a silver garland from our ornament box to encircle it and said, "Now everybody can put their presents on the table."

I had to reach under the bed to retrieve my gifts: two rolls of Life Savers for Papa, a perfumed, dime store necklace for Mama, and a set of dominoes for Fritz. Each was wrapped in butcher-shop paper colored with crayons. Of course, Fritz beat me back to the dining room with his presents: a hankie for Mama, a cigar for Papa and a flat package for me. How I hoped it would be paper dolls!

Papa said, "Fritz, get your violin and I will light our candle in remembrance of Jesus who brought light to the world."

"I walked the full length of the avenue without finding a Christmas tree," Papa said. "Never mind. This year we will have a Christmas table."

First we sang *Silent Night* in German, then *Von Himmel Hoch Da Kam Ich Her (I Came Here From High Heaven)*. Fritz played a waltz he had learned for his recital. Papa pulled out his harmonica and blew *Oh Christmas Tree* while Mama hunted for the Old Maid cards. I was Old Maid most of the time. Later, Mama

treated us to lebkuchen and hazelnut cookies with cocoa. No one in the whole world baked as well as our mother.

When Mama was tucking me in she said, "I know you feel sad not having a Christmas tree, but if God had wanted us to have one, your Papa would have found it. Say your prayers and sleep

> *Halfway home I spotted a discarded Christmas tree. It even had a few pieces of tinsel dangling from the branches. Suddenly, my brother swooped down and put the lower trunk on his shoulder.*

well. Tomorrow morning we will open presents."

After prayers I tried to think of a reason God didn't want us to have a tree.

Christmas was wonderful. After oatmeal and stollen we opened our presents. Fritz got Johnson Racer ice skates, fur mittens and a box of dominoes. I got clamp-on ice skates, a wool cap and paper dolls. Mama and Papa gave each other a capon, which Mama would roast for Christmas dinner.

After church Fritz and I ice-skated at the pond until it was time to go home and eat. We were so tired and hungry that we gobbled our food, stretched out in front of the radio and fell sound asleep. When we awoke there was just time for a snack and we hopped in bed, but I remember Papa saying that we could skate every day during our Christmas vacation.

We walked down the alley coming home from the pond the next afternoon as it gave some shelter from the wind. Halfway home I spotted a discarded Christmas tree. It even had a few pieces of tinsel dangling from the branches.

"Look Fritz, we could ask?" Being older, it was his fate to have to be wiser so he stopped to think. Suddenly, he swooped down and put the lower trunk on his shoulder. I followed, carrying the tip.

At home Mama came out to see our surprise. "Such a nice tree. Well, we have ornaments and lights so bring it in. We'll decorate it before Papa comes home."

What fun we had dolling up that secondhand tree. Mama pointed out that the small ornaments should be hung on the top and the larger ones on the bottom. Among the colored lights she said there must only be three blue ones—in memory of Grandmother, Uncle Karl and Uncle August (her two brothers who were killed in World War I).

Papa was delighted. "Such a wonderful tree must be left up until New Years Day. Kids, you did a fine job." We beamed.

While being tucked in that night I said, "Mama, God wanted us to have a tree after all, didn't he?"

"Yes, it was one of his wonderful, mysterious ways," she said as she smiled and turned out the light. ✶

The Buttermilk Tree

By Lela Dirikson as told to Trula Johnson

Families, farms and fun were simple back around the turn of the century. I, a young farm girl of 12, and my older sister, Ella, 14, were the eldest in a family of nine children.

In 1906 we lived in Durant, Okla., on a small farm of 50 acres, with our parents and grandparents. I recall clearly that particular day, December 23.

Papa, Mama and Pa's parents were working with some livestock in a pasture a few miles away from the house. We nine children were left at home as the day was cold and snow was piled at least a foot deep around our home.

Ellie, a great one for fun and games, said, "Why don't we tie some of those red birthday candles to our Christmas tree? We've got some twine, and that cedar tree is so bare; all it has are kids' drawings and rings of popped corn strung on it. It needs sparkle."

> *Ellie, a great one for fun and games, said, "Why don't we tie some of those red birthday candles to our Christmas tree? That cedar tree is so bare; it needs sparkle."*

Being wary by nature, I shook my head. I wanted to spread thick, white icing on the freshly baked chocolate cake, just warm from the oven. Sweet, spicy smells from the gingerbread cookies, turkey dressing and baked pies filled the country kitchen.

Our job as the oldest girls was to bake while our folks were out doing the farm work. Although it was early, I had already baked fresh bread, two cakes and some cookies. Ellie had helped, but she didn't like cooking, so her mind was wandering to something that was fun.

Hearing her rapid footsteps, I turned to see her excited face as she said, "Aw, the little ones want a prettier tree." They bobbed their heads in agreement. "Come on, help us decorate that plain tree."

She pointed to the tall cedar tree, sturdily braced in a far east corner of the foyer which adjoined the kitchen. The tree had been placed on display close to the three adjoining windows to be seen from the road.

I felt myself weakening, as I did like to spruce up the tree. I looked at Bud, the oldest boy at 10, and he caught my glance.

"You girls know we're not to touch those candles or the matches when the grownups ain't here," he said. He jammed his fists in his faded blue coveralls and stood there, short and stocky.

Ellie just tossed her head, then grinned broadly as she said, "Bud, you and Lela are just old sticks-in-the-mud."

She waved her hand in a wide circle to indicate the tight circle of small children ganged around her. "Guess you want to spoil these little kids' Christmas?" All six little heads nodded in agreement as tears began to well in their midnight blue eyes.

I glanced at their disappointed faces, then I surrendered. "Well, if we are real careful, we might surprise Mama and Papa. They might even like it."

Bud grabbed the long wooden bench and Ellie helped him drag it to the fireplace mantel where the twine, matches and candles were kept. Bud and Ellie passed the items to me and I giggled nervously at the sight of the forbidden objects.

Walking swiftly to the foyer, I started to

unwrap the balled twine and take the candles from their tiny boxes. Bud whipped out his small pocketknife, a gift from last year, and he swiftly sliced the twine into proper lengths for tying.

It was quite a job to get the birthday candles to stand up from the limbs as they were supposed to, but finally we had 30 candles tied to the tree properly. We three oldest ones at last stepped back to admire our handiwork.

"Just beautiful! Aren't you glad we did it?" Ellie exclaimed, with two thin fists dug into her tiny hips. Everyone agreed.

The little ones stared with wide-eyed wonderment as they stood closer to the now-glowing red birthday candles. I imagined that it was our own tiny Christmas mass, and we worshiped it like a shrine.

Time passed and we drifted, two or three at a time, to gather at the huge oilclothed kitchen table to plan our Yuletide gifts for our parents and grandparents. Now distanced from the foyer and still-glowing tree, we exchanged excited plans for the holiday.

Suddenly, the smell of burning cedar branches and tiny gray smoke wisps reached our eyes and noses. Ellie screamed, "The tree's on fire!"

We jumped up, knocking over our benches and chairs. Like little frightened puppies, we bumped into each other.

"Bud, run down the road to Big John's place and tell him to come help us," I screamed. Bud stood frozen to the spot, blue eyes wide with terror.

"Kids, stay back!" Ellie yelled. She ran into the kitchen to get the large family water bucket on its bench by the east wall. Discarding the family water dipper, she dashed to the tree. Stiffening her knees, she braced herself to throw the water at the now-blazing tree.

With a mighty hurl, she heaved the water from the bucket. The water landed to the right of the flames and the fire darted to the left to crawl up the tree.

In seconds the paper cutout dolls, Santa, sleigh and reindeer curled into black crisp ashes. The popcorn balls—scorched, blackened, and now free from their burned twine rings—fell down the charred paths to the floor.

The blaze climbed upward to reach the paper angel perched near the top of the cedar. Speechless, I jumped into action. I dashed to the four-burner wood-burning cookstove. I grabbed

Suddenly, the smell of burning cedar branches and tiny gray smoke wisps reached our eyes and noses. Ellie screamed, "The tree's on fire!"

the large enamel coffee pot still half-full from breakfast that morning.

With two pot holders clutched in my hands, I raced swiftly to the tree, holding the heavy pot. With both feet firmly dug into the floor, I threw that warm coffee dead center to the left side of the flames. Since I was only four feet tall, it failed to reach high enough to do much good.

The sap-filled branches hissed and sputtered. Snaking up still higher, the flames devoured a tiny angel with her hand-stitched white silk dress in seconds. Her carefully braided cotton hair with its pearl-beaded crown burst into flames.

Bud sprang into action as I stood there staring. His stout, muscular legs pumped furiously as he raced to grab the churn standing next to the cabinet, still full of buttermilk from that morning's churning.

Barreling up to just inches from the burning tree, he braced his sturdy legs as he threw that foaming buttermilk at the raging flames.

I grabbed the heavy brown oilcloth separator cover from the stand and beat at the flames furiously. The fire hissed, snapped and then was smothered as the attack increased. Suddenly, the tree crumpled, then fell to its side. It smelled like a wet puppy and looked like a dirty white ghost.

A roomful of weeping children escorted the tree out back through the kitchen door to roll it in the wet snow. Our hands were wrapped in heavy towels to prevent blisters. We chanted a prayer for the tree's soul. We knew that it would go directly to tree heaven as soon as our prayers ended.

Afterward, we walked single file back into the foyer and stared at the kitchen floor. We had to clean up before our folks returned for their noon meal.

The window in the foyer was a total mess. Buttermilk tinged with black, sooty fire wastes pooled on the braided brown rug; it looked like it was ruined. Coffee stains clung to the yellow-and-white striped wallpaper, and we knew it would never be pretty again.

The smell of buttermilk, coffee and smoke filled the air. We sniffed back tears, wiping our leaking noses with quick swipes. We clung to each other as we wept our young hearts out.

Suddenly, the back kitchen door opened and in stepped our parents and grandparents. I prayed hard that the floor would open up and swallow me whole. Papa's dark brown eyes narrowed to dangerous slits as he covered the distance to reach us. His eyes moved to take in the damage showing in the kitchen and foyer.

Mama's usually warm blue eyes stared at first one and then the other's shamed faces. Grandma and Grandpa stepped to Papa's side as he stood grim-faced and silent.

Papa questioned, "Ellie, I saw the burned tree and melted birthday candles outside in the snow. You're the oldest; and Lela, no doubt, helped to cause this mess."

Ellie, grabbing for my icy hand, stepped closer to me and whispered, "It's my fault, and I'll take the licking for all of us." Tears ran down her face, dropping into her tiny, crocheted white collar. No one spoke for the longest time.

I jerked my head up from its shamed position when Grandpa spoke to Papa, breaking the silence: "John, we both know these children did a bad thing by playing with matches and candles when we were not here." Grandpa's brown eyes held Papa's gaze steadily.

Grandpa paused, cleared his throat, then added, "They've learned a bitter lesson about fire today. They'll have no Christmas tree this year." Papa continued to stare at his father silently.

Papa ducked his head, looked then at Mama, then he stepped close to his father to touch his shoulder. A look of trust and respect seemed to settle in his eyes. He knelt and held out his long, strong arms to all of us. We rushed wildly to receive hugs and kisses from all of them. The grownups pitched in and we cleaned up that mess together.

Well, I am now a centenarian. I tell this buttermilk tree story over and over to each generation as they gather to celebrate Christmas.

My memory isn't as good as it used to be, but I can still smell that scorched buttermilk, coffee and smoke-filled house. It's somewhat like a family coat of arms.

But, most importantly, our family's love and trust for each other commemorate each Christmas—and I'll never forget that warm feeling. ✱

Blue Junk

By Audrey Theurer

This is the year, the year we divide all the Christmas trimmings with the married children and have a beautifully planned symbol of the season.

"Let's have a flocked tree," my husband said, "trimmed in all one color, just for fun."

"What color?" asked a new daughter-in-law, and was startled at the laughter from all my sons.

"It will have to be blue," one said, "or she won't play."

"She won't have a tree she can't hang her blue junk on," another son explained, and while the girls waited expectantly, I brought forth the small box that holds the two tarnished and faded blue ornaments. I could not get young people to realize that these small globes hold all the Christmas that one middle-aged lady ever had.

In 1935, at the old Main Street grade school in Dallas, we placed a bare fir tree in the corner of the first-grade room. Each child could bring from home two decorations, Mrs. Ruth explained to us. That way the tree would be decorated for our Christmas party. It would have to be the grandest tree in the whole school, because we were the smallest children, because the principal would be there, and because we would be excused an hour early.

This is exactly the way I remem-

ber it. That tree standing bare, then trimmed, is clear to me yet, and I can't for the life of me remember the party or the principal.

All the way home, I worried about the way my mother would react. Our Christmas things were way up in the attic, and my dad was working away from home. All that long weekend we waited, just in case he might get home; he didn't. I cried myself to sleep under the covers that Sunday night with visions of that bare tree the last thought I had.

In the way of mothers, she followed me out the door the next morning and put our movie dime deep into my mitten. (Mom and all four of us kids went to the movie for 10 cents on Wednesday night, if Dad wasn't home.) She told me to stop at the variety store on my way to school and pick out two 5-cent decorations. If Dad got home, we would have movie money, and if he didn't, we could stay home and pop corn.

There were at least 10 million jewel-like objects on the counter of the store, the largest selections marked 5 cents each. The counter sloped from high in the back to just about my eye level in the front. Bedded deep in loose straw they were all shapes, sizes and colors.

I was so excited there were goose bumps going up my arms and down my legs. The dime

I was so excited there were goose bumps going up my arms and down my legs. The dime clutched tightly in my hand, I walked up and down that aisle on my tiptoes at least a dozen times.

clutched tightly in my hand, I walked up and down that aisle on my tiptoes at least a dozen times. That was the very first money I ever had to spend and I wasn't going to make a mistake.

The first one I chose was a cluster of grapes about 2 inches long, the shades of blue blending into a serious color that glittered when you turned it to the light. Diamond rings, new babies and expensive cars have passed through my hands since then, but I have never had the same feeling of complete surrender.

The second bauble was no larger but chosen quickly when the school bell rang three blocks away. It was pale blue and had a white design of mistletoe.

They winked at me from the branches of "our tree" all that week and then were carried

home, one in each hand, to be the only new trims on that Christmas tree in that Depression year.

Santa Claus came to Dallas that year on a fire engine. Since the stores were small and the town not large, there had been no Santas sprinkled about; our only previous contact with the old gent had been briefly on the radio. Our children miss so much with saturation.

We each had a visit with him and someone gave us each a sack containing candy, an orange and a toy. There were girl sacks and boy sacks, and four of us danced home in the cold, quite sure we were the luckiest kids in the world. Those ornaments on the tree made up for the long brown cotton stockings I had received instead of the white ones I had my heart set on.

The blue ornaments followed through my childhood. They were two of only four left the year the Christmas tree fell over all by itself in a room with five boisterous children. During my teens they missed being replaced because of a war that made buying new ones impossible.

When we were planning the Christmas tree in Philomath for our first son, Dad helped me unpack all the trimming at his house in Portland after a full Thanksgiving dinner.

"Is that what I got all this stuff down for?" he stormed when I found what I wanted at the bottom of the last box. "If you need new stuff, I'll get you some," and he reached for his billfold. I tried to explain that they held Dallas, Clatskanie, brown stockings, eggnog, a first kiss, giggles and many other things. He listened and chewed his cigar but I'm not sure he really understood. I haven't tried to explain it again; it is just there.

There have been 25 Christmas seasons since then, shared with family, three sons, new daughters, and this year a new grandson. The flocked white tree trimmed in blue will be up on the table to stand out of the reach of yet another child, and in its uppermost branches will be two of the most beautiful blue trinkets in the entire world. ✳

Since the stores were small and the town not large, there had been no Santas sprinkled about; our only previous contact with the old gent had been briefly on the radio. We each had a visit with him and someone gave us a sack containing candy, an orange and a toy.

That Special Tree

By John Forrest

J ohnnie? John!" The sharp tone of the teacher's voice pierced my thoughts and the vision of the family gathered 'round the Christmas tree in their wilderness cabin faded quickly from my mind.

Although our Friday afternoon story time was over, I had remained caught in the author's magic web. Grinning sheepishly, I ducked my head and rummaged in my desk, ears burning at the sound of giggling from my second-grade classmates.

Miss Campbell had been reading a story about a pioneer family's Christmas. In their struggle to get ready for their first winter in the wilderness, they had forgotten all about celebrating. Then the youngest child, a boy about my age, slips away on a special mission. When they discover he's missing, his worried family fears the worst, but our hero arrives home safely, dragging a beautiful evergreen up to the door of their cabin. It was the stuff that dreams are made of!

Class dismissed, but on the walk home I discovered that my friend and classmate Jimmy Davidson shared my feelings. Scuffing our way through the ankle-deep snow, we marveled at the boy's quest and how, forgotten by all, he had become the hero. *Why not us?* we thought.

Jim and I lived on the outskirts of the city. Our family had moved there after Dad's discharge from the Air Force, in the spring of 1946; and this would be a special Christmas for us, our first together since his return from the war. Jim's family arrived right after we did and he and I hit it off immediately. Like Tom Sawyer and Huck Finn, we spent much of our time roaming the tracts of bush that surrounded our homes and exploring the old estate that was nearby.

It was decided. We would get Christmas trees for our families; the best Christmas trees ever! Saturday morning dawned clear and crisp, with a light dusting of new snow

The gate was open and the icy wheel ruts that stretched down the sloping lane made a perfect toboggan track. It was time to have some fun!

sprinkled on the landscape. With Jim towing his toboggan and me shouldering Dad's saw, we started our search. Every flash of green caught our eye and we hurried from tree to tree, trying to pick the best ones. We did not have much success.

Although we found plenty of trees to choose from, none were just right and there was always a better tree "just over there." Our enthusiasm was beginning to wane, when we reached the imposing fieldstone pillars that guarded the entrance to the Rattray Estate.

It was decided. We would get Christmas trees for our families; the best Christmas trees ever!

The gate was open and the icy wheel ruts that stretched down the sloping lane made a perfect toboggan track. It was time to have some fun! I hopped on and Jim pushed off. We slid down the slope, gathering speed like a bobsled.

Too much speed! Rocketing into the curve at the bottom of the hill, we jumped the track, climbed a snowbank and were dumped into a drift! Rolling out of the wreckage I looked around to get my bearings. There before me, cloaked in Christmas-card mantles of snow, stood our trees. They were perfect!

The rest of that day was spent hidden under the protecting lower boughs of those trees, struggling to saw through trunks that were almost as thick as our legs. We finished cutting and our prizes toppled. Now to get them home!

Jim towed his tree on the toboggan and I skidded mine along the snow-covered shoulder of the road. Cars slid past, flashing their lights in the gathering dusk and giving us a wide berth. The street lamps blinked on.

Strings of colored lights began to twinkle on the houses and a gentle snow started to fall. With smiles lighting our faces, we went our separate ways and I quickened my pace in eager anticipation of the welcome I would receive.

The front of our house was bathed in red and green by the floodlights on the lawn. Resting the tree against the porch, I rang the bell and stood down proudly, beside my gift.

Mom opened the storm door and peered out. A look of relief crossed her face, followed quickly by one of surprise and concern.

"John!" she exclaimed. "Where did you get that tree?" Dad appeared behind her, put his hand to his forehead and groaned, "Oh, no."

My heart sank! It was not the reaction I expected.

"It's our Christmas tree!" I replied. "I cut it just for us. I thought you'd like it," I squeaked, my eyes filling with tears.

Dad came to the rescue. "We do, John," he said, nudging Mother. "Come inside and tell us about it."

I brightened a little and hurried up the steps. Mom stopped me on the way by, hugged me hard and whispered, "It's a wonderful tree." Over dinner, I poured out the tale of the pioneer boy, and my search for a special tree for our Christmas. Little did I know how special that tree was.

You see, I had presented my parents with a beautiful blue spruce, which just happened to be one of the matching markers that flanked the driveway to the estate.

We decorated that spruce and celebrated our Christmas beneath it. Perfectly shaped, thick, bushy and tinged with blue, it was transformed into a shimmering cone of multicolored light. It was magical.

It wasn't until my parents began telling the story to friends that I fully understood the reason for their reluctant response to my gift. The Rattrays were understanding. They settled for an apology and our help in replacing the trees.

That was the last time I provided the family fir; however, retelling the story of "John's tree" has become a Christmas tradition.

Jim moved away the following autumn and our paths never crossed again. But to this day, the sight of a blue spruce frosted with snow brings back images of that childhood quest. And, I fondly recall how that special tree filled a little boy's heart with joy and provided our family with a cherished Christmas memory. ✶

The First Lighted Christmas Tree

By Harriet E. Gowey

Of course, the first Christmas trees were lighted by candles, and I am not talking about those, although I remember them very well. My own early trees were never candlelit, for the practice was very dangerous, and resulted in many home fires.

My father would never allow it, but there was a large family across the street from my early childhood home in Pennsylvania who always had a candlelit tree. Each of their many children was allowed to bring a little friend on Christmas night to witness their candlelighting ceremony.

The first such lights we had on our own tree were bought for the Christmas of 1911 and cost $8 for a string of only eight little globes.

I was always chosen by one of the little girls, and so I got to sit on the floor in the living room with my Christmas doll in my arms, while the father of the family lit the wax tapers on their 10-foot tree with a special taper which was also used for lighting the gaslights. When the last candle was lit, he would take up a position in the dining room doorway, a pail of water on each side in case the tree should catch fire.

The mother took her place at the piano and played Christmas carols as long as the candles burned. All the children sang, and I am sure none of us ever forgot those bright moments. I am sure I never have, although all this was 70 years ago!

The tree which I remember later was in a downtown hotel in Philadelphia. It was the Hotel Bellevue-Stratford, and my father took my mother and me there as part of our annual Christmas treat. It was his yearly custom to take us into Philadelphia on an evening just before Christmas to see the lighted stores, and to do a little last-minute shopping. We took a local train, known as the Redding Road, from the suburb where we lived, and it was always part of the fun to stop in somewhere for ice cream and cake.

This year, which was the Christmas of 1905, he took us into the Bellevue-Stratford for refreshments, for he knew about their lighted trees. They were not real trees, actually, but were made to resemble them by twining the pillars in the hotel dining room with ropes of greenery, and then twisting ropes of small colored lights in with them. The effect was very pretty, and attracted many guests to the hotel, for these were the first tiny colored lights that anyone in Philadelphia had seen.

The first such lights that we had on our own home tree were bought for the Christmas of 1911, after we had moved to Denver, Colo. My mother protested their purchase as an extravagance, for the lights cost $8 for a string of only eight little globes, but I was delighted and got a real thrill out of admitting the many strangers who came to our door and asked if they could come in and see "the tree with the electric lights" which they had heard we had.

Of course, the tiny globes were different from the ones we have today. They ended in a sharp point and were very durable. In fact, I have two globes left from that early string, and they still light, after all the years!

This is the tree to which I refer, my first "all-electric" one. It still glows in my memory and is not displaced by the trees which I have nowadays, whose beauty is enjoyed by the married children and grandchildren who gather around them. ✶

Chapter Five

Christmas on the Front

I'll be home for Christmas." So went the song and so went the hopes and dreams of many young American men and women through the four long years of World War II. From the European Theater to the South Pacific, from defense plants to the family farm—no family went without knowing the sacrifice for world security.

And, while we all gave willingly to the cause, we also knew the profound loss. Many lost fathers, sons, husbands, uncles, cousins and friends. Those who didn't knew at least the meaning of lost time. Years for children to be without fathers. Months waiting for furloughs. Weeks waiting for word from loved ones. Days that seemed like decades. No time of the year was it more apparent than at Christmas.

"I'll be home for Christmas."

It was a promise that largely went unfulfilled for most of us. While the war raged on, we found the true meaning of melancholy. Even when we knew for a certainty that our loved ones were safe—and we rarely knew that—their absence at the Yuletide season made each wartime Christmas that much harder to bear.

How many mothers ached for word from sons? How many sweethearts and wives looked for a special V-Mail note? And how many times did

we wish for the war to cease, especially around the season of peace?

"I'll be home for Christmas"—and we knew it was ultimately true. Because those who spent Christmas on the front were kept close to the hearts of those who spent Christmas on the home front. Though thousands of miles apart, separated by oceans and continents, the prayers of every family gathered around a holiday table were directed toward all of the empty chairs in kitchens and dining rooms around the nation.

And we all knew the meaning of the words of that favorite song: "I'll be home for Christmas—if only in my dreams." ✶

Have a Coca-Cola = Merry Christmas

...or how Americans spread the holiday spirit overseas

Your American fighting man loves his lighter moments. Quick to smile, quick to enter the fun, he takes his home ways with him where he goes...makes friends easily. *Have a "Coke"*, he says to stranger or friend, and he spreads the spirit of good will throughout the year. And throughout the world Coca-Cola stands for *the pause that refreshes,*—has become the high-sign of the friendly-hearted.

*   *   *

Our fighting men are delighted to meet up with Coca-Cola many places overseas. Coca-Cola has been a globe-trotter "since way back when". Even with war, Coca-Cola today is being bottled right on the spot in over 35 allied and neutral nations.

It's natural for popular names to acquire friendly abbreviations. That's why you hear Coca-Cola called "Coke".

Coca-Cola
-the global high-sign

One Italian Christmas

By Gene Brewington

ver 50 years ago, Christmas Eve 1944, we were in some nameless village high in the Apennine mountains of Italy. We had seen a hundred villages just like it, as we had fought, clawed and died on our way up the Italian peninsula.

We had been trying to take this village for three days. After days of shelling by the artillery, and bombing by the "fly-boys," we had finally gained control. There were not three untouched houses remaining. The rest were complete or partial piles of rubble.

We moved into the village just before dusk. Outposts were placed, and perimeter guards were posted. An occasional incoming artillery shell was the only sign of the enemy. We were all dead on our feet. No hot meal for three days. No bath for a week.

Being a non-com, I was volunteered as sergeant of the guard. It was about 3 a.m., and I was checking my guard posts. Needless to say, I was down in the dumps; it was Christmas Eve, my third away from my family. Tonight there was no tree, no presents and probably not even a Santa Claus. Thousands of miles from home. Bitterly cold. No one cared whether I lived or died—not even me.

As I picked my way through, over and around the rubble, I was constantly alert. The soldier who survives in battle develops a sixth sense. As I passed a large pile of rubble that had once been a house, I thought I heard a moan. It couldn't be. Nothing could be alive in that pile of trash. Listening more closely, I heard it again. With my tommy gun ready, I listened more carefully. I finally ascertained from whence the noise came.

As I carefully moved rocks and pieces of timber, the crying became more distinct. I could not use a light, but with help from a sliver of moonlight, I finally saw a small crumpled body beneath the rubble. After a few minutes of silent work, I reached in and pulled out a little Italian girl. She was perhaps 3 or 4 years old. She was hysterical. Although covered with dirt,

All kinds of toys appeared. Even a doll, who could say "Ma-ma."

she appeared to be in fair shape.

I picked her up and headed for the medics, who were in one of the few still-standing buildings. Easing through the temporary blackout curtains, I deposited her on an examining table. I told one of the medics to clean her up and see if she had anything broken, and that I would be back later.

I returned in about an hour. They had washed her up and combed her hair. She only had a few abrasions, nothing serious. They had given her water and food, and she was calmer.

She did not protest when I picked her up and wrapped her in my overcoat. My platoon had taken over a partially damaged mill house. Feeling my way through the darkness, I located my sleeping bag and crawled in, boots and all. I cuddled the little girl in my arms, and zipped up the bag. She was soon fast asleep.

The grapevine works fast in the Army. It was not long after daylight when a runner shook me awake. "Report to the Old Man immediately."

The "Old Man" must have been at least 30 years old. Leaving the waif under the care of another soldier, I reported to the C.O. His first words were: "Sergeant, I hear you have been fraternizing with the enemy, and had a female in your sleeping bag last night. Yes or no?"

I explained as best I could.

"Dangit, Sergeant, you know we can't have civilians in camp with us," he replied. "You will have to get rid of her."

"Yes, Sir. I will get rid of her, at once—Sir. Shall I shoot her—Sir?"

"Don't be sarcastic, Sergeant. You can keep her today, but tomorrow you can take my jeep and driver, and take her to that convent we passed about 20 miles back."

"Yes, Sir," I replied, grinning to myself.

He dismissed me and I started for the door, but he halted me. "Just a minute, Sarge." Digging through his duffel bag, he came up with a stuffed teddy bear. Looking back, it was laughable that an "old man" would carry a teddy bear. It looked brand-new. He said that he was saving it for his daughter, when he got home. As he handed me the toy, did I see a tear in the old so-and-so's eye? It couldn't be. He was tough as a boot and twice as tall.

When I got back to my sleeping bag, she was awake and being entertained by half of the company. There were always a few soldiers around who could speak Italian. They had learned her name was Lisa. Her parents were somewhere in the rubble. *"Morte! Morte!"*

Every man in the company must have visited Lisa that day. The company tailor, who doubled as a 74mm gunner, had whipped her up a dress and a jacket. He had even made her underclothes, GI in color.

I will never know where they came from, but all kinds of toys appeared. Even a doll, who could say "Ma-ma." Candy and fruit. All from a dirty, stinking, unkempt bunch of dogfaces, any one of whom could—and would—kill without blinking an eye. More love was given and received that Christmas Day so long ago than I have ever seen, before or since.

As the jeep pulled away the next morning, Lisa, in her new GI uniform, cuddled in my lap as two duffel bags of goodies in back jostled over the rough roads. I thought of the gifts of the Magi, so long ago. Maybe there is a spark of love in the world, in spite of man's inhumanity to man. Maybe there really is a Santa Claus. ✶

Christmas, War & Turnips

By George T. and Thresa B. Ziak

Our Christmas dinner has always been traditional through the years along with one special treat that is usually very visual and odd. It is always noticed by guests and invariably someone asks, "Why do you have a raw turnip with a pocketknife stuck into it as the center attraction on your table?"

The family members have anticipated their reaction to this peculiarity and smile at one another. Finally one comments, "Well now, that is a story that Dad loves to tell every Christmas." Everyone turns their attention to Dad and he begins:

✯✯✯

I was shipped overseas as a rifleman in World War II. I arrived in Liverpool, England, on a troop ship in the middle of the winter. A bunch of us soldiers were whisked into France and up to the front lines. I joined what was left of the 424th Infantry Regiment of the 106th Infantry Division at Malmédy, Belgium. That was my first contact with the enemy.

When I joined the regiment it was during the Battle of the Belgium Bulge. (It was called that because the Germans had made a pincer movement and created a bulge in our line, hence it was called the Belgium Bulge.) Another soldier and I joined the outfit the same evening and we were welcomed with open arms, as our company had been beaten down to 68 men from a normal strength of 200 men.

The next morning we kicked off and from

Months went by; we spent our time in foxholes surrounded by heavy snow and freezing cold and no heat of any kind. No fires were allowed.

that day on it was push, push, push through the dragon teeth and pillboxes of the Siegfried Line of the Germans.

Months went by; we spent our time in foxholes surrounded by heavy snow and freezing cold and no heat of any kind. No fires were allowed. We would scrape the tallow off the rations and throw that part away and eat the cold beef stew. It tasted terrible and we were miserable.

During the daylight hours I happened to spot a deserted farm that had a turnip patch. When night came, I decided to crawl out to it under the cover of darkness and dig up a few turnips. I did and crawled back to the foxhole. The turnips were frozen so we got our pocket knives out and cut the frozen part off and ate the core with gusto. You can't imagine how wonderful and delicious it tasted. To have a fresh vegetable after months of C-rations was really a treat. Then and there I vowed that if I ever got out of the war alive, I would celebrate the turnip every Christmas.

✯✯✯

As he talked Dad peeled and sliced the turnip and when he was done, he passed the plate of sliced turnip to everyone at the table. Dad held up his slice and made a toast, "To the turnip and world peace. Merry Christmas, everyone."

Somehow the ordinary turnip was so much more delectable and the perfect entrée to our Christmas dinner. ✶

Christmas on The Liberty

By Hannah Lords

It was December of 1944, with the world still caught in the grip of World War II. Sue White was one of six Army nurses sailing stateside aboard a Liberty ship. She and two other nurses were returning home as patients; the other three were being discharged after completing their tour of duty overseas.

Jungle rot, a common affliction in the tropics, had been troubling Sue for months, but still it was necessary for her to serve in the capacity for which she had been trained. The Liberty was loaded with wounded service personnel. They must be cared for until they could receive the specialized care each would need when they arrived in the States.

The Navy corpsmen gave excellent care, but still there were not enough hands to fill all the needs. The nurses were all pressed into service, even those who were ill themselves.

The corpsmen worked nights; the nurses worked days. There were six wards. Sue was in charge of the hold where the patients suffering mental or emotional dysfunctions were berthed.

Christmas was approaching. Normally Sue was able to remain in a positive frame of mind, but now she felt her spirits sink during the grim days and nights they sailed through the dark Pacific waters. When her ear infection resisted all available treatment at Finchaven, New Guinea, she was finally able to persuade the doctors to allow her to return to the States for help.

Now as Christmas approached she knew the letters and gifts from home, intended to brighten her holidays and bring cheer from loved ones, would most likely never reach her. Sue's mail, along with the mail of patients and colleagues alike, was on the way to the posts they had left, while they were headed in the opposite direction.

It didn't help matters that lights could not be used. The hold was as dark in daylight as it was at night. On board another ship to her post in Australia, Sue had experienced a torpedo alert. Nothing had changed in that respect. It was necessary to practice the same precautions. She had to develop the ability to find her way around the dark wards by feeling with her hands, and remembering always to step up and over doorways.

The awful darkness Sue's patients had to endure in the wards concerned her. She found herself spending more and more of her free time taking small, manageable groups up on deck for a bit of light and air. Those few precious moments meant a lot to them. The tension they were under was never more clearly indicated than when one of her patients jumped overboard one day. Fortunately he was a good swimmer.

When he was pulled to safety Sue asked, "Why did you jump?"

"I saw you wave your hand and I thought you meant to abandon ship," he replied. He had mistaken her pointing out something in the water for a signal he was to abandon ship!

As the days before Christmas grew fewer Sue began to feel an acute sense of loss and apprehension. That Christmas, out of all the days of the year, should go by unheeded and unheralded

She felt an acute sense of loss and apprehension.

was unthinkable. It was no comfort to see this same sense of malaise affecting her fellow travelers. Then when it seemed patients and crew alike had struck their darkest hour, someone said, "Hey, why can't we have Christmas?"

"Why not?" someone else asked. "But how?"

No one knew how, but hope sprang to life, first in one heart, then another. Soon it seemed everyone on the ship was caught up in the thrill of bringing Christmas into the lives of the suffering patients, and consequently into their own lives as well.

The first call that went out was for cigarette packages. The cellophane would make wonderful, sparkling ornaments.

To the ship's cooks went a request to save all can lids. These same cooks would not spare in their efforts to produce an abundant supply of holiday fare.

The ship's carpenter went into action, making and painting an 18 x 9-inch sign for each of the six wards. For Sue's ward he made a sign with "Christmas Greetings" painted in bright, bold colors. He also made the individual letters in the words "MERRY CHRISTMAS." These were painted red and tied in such a way that they swung gracefully as they were carried from ward to ward.

Little by little everyone was caught up in the warmth and enthusiasm found only in the giving of themselves. The ship's crew made Christmas trees by stringing coat hangers together to form branches. The nurses decorated the trees with the glistening ornaments fashioned from the

cellophane saved from cigarette packages.

Shining coils were laboriously formed by cutting spirals from can lids with tin snips borrowed from the carpenter's shop. This turned out to be a bloody battle when tender hands were cut on the sharp edges, but these scars were soon forgotten when the spirals shone forth from the coat hanger branches.

And then it was Christmas Eve! There was a stillness among those gathered in their respective wards to contemplate, to draw inward for a moment and savor this special place in time.

Sue wondered if others were asking themselves, as people do everywhere: *Is this the end? Must I now put away all the hopes and elation that led up to this point? Must I lay aside the warmth, the fellowship, the remembering of Christmases that went before?*

"Let's sing," a voice spoke into the darkness.

"Naw, I ain't gonna sing," another avowed.

But sing they did! One or two at first, then, with gentle urging, another. A young man brought out his hand organ and started to play, and soon the ship rang with the voices of those who found Christmas, even in their great darkness.

What would those shepherds on that distant Judean hillside think, had they known Christ's birth still had the power, nearly 2,000 years later, to cause people to look beyond their circumstance, and joyfully sacrifice in their giving to and loving of their fellow man?

So it was in the hearts and lives of those who cared for the wounded and hurting on the Liberty ship that Christmas of 1944.

And so it is today, for both Sue and her husband, Dave, who still practice the custom established in Sue's life almost 50 years ago.

When Sue left the ship for the hospital a few days after that memorable Christmas, she took with her the sign made for her ward. She would undergo treatment for the next three months for her badly infected ears, but she kept that sign and it has been a part of her and Dave's Christmases throughout the years they raised their family.

It is their custom still to hang it where those gathered might see and remember. Christmas isn't about the magnitude and multitude of gifts received. It is in the giving of self for the blessing of others. ✷

The Christmas Card I'll Never Forget

By Frances M. Callahan

On Dec. 24, 1943, I received a Christmas card which I will never forget.

Two generations have been added to our family in the intervening years; yet, each year when Christmas cards start coming, time seems to telescope like an old-fashioned collapsible drinking cup, and vivid memories of that long-ago holiday season flood my mind.

Christmas cards started arriving in mid-December of 1943. Each day, as I returned home from my job at an aircraft factory, the mail was uppermost in my mind. Anxiously I would riffle through the envelopes hoping to find one bearing a Fleet P.O. return address. At their respective homes, my parents and two sisters were all keeping equally close tabs on their mailboxes, for it had been more than two months since any of us had heard from my only brother.

If any of us were to find that long-hoped-for and prayed-for envelope in our mail, we didn't really expect it would hold a Christmas card. All we wanted, with all our hearts, was a short note of any kind, or a V-mail letter scrawled in Bud's inimitable hand.

True, there had been other long periods without word from him since he, along with thousands of other Marines, had stormed the beaches at Guadalcanal on Aug. 7, 1942. But the thought of not knowing where or how he was at Christmastime seemed nearly unbearable.

Yet day after long December day went by without that envelope arriving. In our phone calls to each other, the results were always negative. As the family's anxiety grew, we tried to be supportive of each other with the old cliché that "No news is good news." But of course that much-overworked saying was of small consolation in view of the war news coming from the South Pacific in those dreadful days.

By the 22nd of December the influx of holiday mail

had dwindled to a mere trickle. On the 23rd only one greeting card arrived, and it was not the right one. My heart sank; my hopes vanished. Christmas just wouldn't be Christmas this year. Bud was a career Marine in his ninth year of service, and this would be the first Christmas there had been no card or holiday letter from him. We are a family with strong ties; we keep in touch. Were we another family destined to be ravaged by the war? I slept very little that night, and went to work the next day with a heavy heart.

Not knowing where or how he was at Christmastime seemed nearly unbearable.

On my return from work I found the mailbox filled with envelopes. Apparently the post office's campaign to "Mail early!" had been ignored by quite a few of my friends! After taking off my coat, I picked up the sheaf of letters which I had laid on the table when I came into the house.

Then, there it was—the third envelope down in the stack. I would have recognized the handwriting among the hundred others!

Breathing a quick, prayerful sigh of relief, my anxious fingers quickly tore open the long-awaited envelope. Pulling out the card, I barely noticed the picture on the front; I was searching for the personal note which I was confident I would find on the card itself or on an enclosed piece of paper. Our family never sends birthday, Christmas or other greeting cards that are simply signed!

Opening the card, I found my brother's short but welcome note on the left portion of the center crease. It was dated Dec. 12 and as I read the words I was still very aware that during war, battles are fought and men die in much less time than had elapsed since he had written the card.

But he had been well when the brief note was written, and he had said, "Can't tell you where I am," which seemed to imply that he

was no longer on Guadalcanal. We would learn months later that his company had indeed been moved to another island in the South Pacific.

My eyes brimmed with tears as I finished reading Bud's note. I breathed a silent prayer of thanks for his well-being, and I beseeched God for his continued safety, and to bring a swift end to the horrible war with its costly sacrifice of mankind. My heart filled with compassion for all the war-bereaved who would never again receive a letter or a Christmas card from loved ones who had made the supreme sacrifice. Encompassed in these agonizing thoughts, I wept uncontrollably and unashamedly for a long time.

Finally, when the flood of tears had passed, I picked up the card again and really saw it for the first time. On the half opposite from where my brother had written was a replica of a sleeve patch of the 1st Marines, Guadalcanal: a blue diamond with a large red numeral one standing vertically from the top to bottom points of the diamond. Small white letters reading "Guadalcanal" were in a perpendicular line in the large numeral one. Printed in black and superimposed over the patch design were the words "Peace on earth, good will toward men."

After reading these words, words as old as Christmas itself, I turned to the picture of the Marine patrol on the front of the card. It seemed an enigmatic combination: a scene of war with a message of peace. For a brief moment, I felt that it was sacrilegious.

Then, studying the picture, I raised my eyes from the figure of the Marine patrolling through the jungle night to the Christmas star. I suddenly thought, *Where could there be a greater and more sincere wish for "peace on earth and good will toward men" than in the hearts of military men from a peace-loving nation like our own? Who is better qualified to know the true blessings of peace than those who are suffering the horrors of war?*

In the many Christmas seasons which have come and gone since 1943, I have never received a more unforgettable Christmas card. To me, the picture on it is as soul-stirring as the famous news photo of the flag-raising on Iwo Jima. I have often wished that the picture on

Continued on Page 115

Ever that same Star...

That star has never failed us yet—it won't fail us now. The darker the night, the brighter it seems to burn.

It is a beacon of hope—a promise of the secure new tomorrow for which mankind is striving.

Swifter than any plane, swifter than radio, swifter than the thoughts of men, its spirit travels around this earth—carrying, even against the distractions of war, its age-old message of hope and assurance.

And that star's bright gleam reflects the greeting sent across the miles to the ends of the world—a greeting to every man and woman in the service of their country—a greeting from your neighbors—from your friends—from all America.

Another year may be different—let's hope it is. Let's keep our eyes on that star with its promise of peace—another year and another Yuletide when again we will hear your familiar voice shouting—"Merry Christmas!"

THE STUDEBAKER CORPORATION
Builders of aircraft engines for the Boeing Flying Fortress

A 1919 Christmas Furlough

By George Montgomery

"F all in the furlough party!" The 1 o'clock assembly bell, followed by those words, was met with loud cheers as we formed two ranks in the Seaman Gunner School Study Hall to receive furlough papers granting a 13-day leave over the Christmas holidays. Names were read alphabetically. With the last, we marched by twos down the walk and through the 11th Street gate to be on our way, leaving those who so graciously had volunteered to carry on in our absence. Some of those we left behind lived too far away; some had no homes to go to; some remained for other reasons. Special privileges had been granted, however; there would be no studies, and only the regular routine would be carried out during the interval.

A round of social activities had taken place, including a dance for the departing April class. The night before a Christmas dinner had been served by the local Red Cross in appreciation for our assistance during their Saturday surplus sales, and our volunteer M.P. duty at their Saturday night dances.

With some others, I walked over to Eighth Street and boarded a streetcar that would take me directly to Union Station. Upon arrival I began checking train departures.

The Armistice was just a year old, and that, together with an advancement in rating scarcely a month earlier, made me somewhat impetuous. I agreed to accompany our section leader to New York. Traveling across town from the Pennsylvania Station to Grand Central, he was able to make the Springfield train, change in Hartford, and arrive home in Putnam about midnight. I just missed the Gilt Edge Express to Boston which would have taken me directly to New London, and now faced a long wait until well after midnight.

A light supper in an adjoining restaurant appeased my appetite; some six hours had passed since the noontime meal at the barracks. As I returned to the terminal, the Times Square lights in all their holiday glory held no appeal, for it was bitter cold. Consequently there was no alternative but to return to the waiting room for the duration.

The only way to break the monotony was an occasional stroll around the terminal. The hands on that large clock over the newsstand seemed to stand still. It seemed like eternity before the voice of a train announcer called out "Shore Line to Boston," naming the stations in order. Being first in line, I was first through the gate. Entering the nearest coach, I found a seat, deposited my bag on the overhead rack, then removed both coat and hat and settled down for the remainder of the trip.

It was snowing as we emerged from the tunnel, and the snow seemed to have increased when we stopped at 125th Street. From there on I fell asleep, only vaguely aware of the stations called until reaching New Haven. It was about an hour's run from there to New London. There would be a short delay while changes were made from the electric to steam locomotives, but once in motion, when I heard, "New London next stop," I decided it best to remain awake.

As we pulled into Union Station, the snow had decreased somewhat. It being between 4 and 4:30, there was ample time for coffee at the Star Restaurant before the ferry would arrive from Groton. Warmed with coffee and reinforced with some doughnuts, I made my way to the New London Ferry House to await the ferry's arrival. This would take me to the Groton side, where a seven-mile hike lay between me and home.

There were modern conveyances for hire, but I feared that in that weather, together with the early morning hour, the reception would not

have been very pleasant; and there being no phone out at the farm, there was no alternative but to pull on rubbers, change flat hat to watch cap, and with pea jacket collar turned up, set out to brave the elements.

The last street light was at Church Street and from there on it was over hills, through swamps and wildernesses, past a few farms scattered along the way. An east wind blew snow over icy places in the road; one misstep could result in a serious injury, and at that hour, there would be no one to lend a hand.

Reaching the old Toll Gate House, I knew that I was about halfway home. Some 50 paces beyond was the final resting place of two of my forebears, under the large pine in a little cemetery. Had they been hovering about, they probably would have been quoting Shakespeare: "What fools these mortals be."

About the only time I was concerned was when I reached the yellow barn just across from the Skunk Lane Road. The barn was believed to be a rendezvous for tramps and hoboes. My mother had written of some robberies having taken place in that general vicinity; there were times that I wished for eyes on all sides. All was quiet in passing, but just beyond, a rabbit stomping its feet startled me out of a year's growth.

After that, the same quiet atmosphere prevailed. There were no lights at Daboll's store, and but a few in Center Groton. John Haley's dog barked as I turned onto the north road, as did Gus Gray's at the open gateway just before Madison's Hill. The old adage, "Ignore a dog or a snake and there's less chance it'll harm you," proved true; I wasn't too far past when he retreated, no doubt seeking warmer quarters.

From here on, it was all upgrade; and in places, the snow had drifted, making walking more difficult. But being so close now, there was nothing to do but press on.

Through the lighted window, I could see the Watrous children around their Christmas tree. Their radiant faces filled with the joy of the occasion brought to mind the first Christmas of my recollection, when Uncle Reuben Lester, in that very same house, had given me a pencil and jackknife. These two treasures so dear to a boy's heart, together with the spirit with which they were given, somehow made clear the true meaning of Christmas, even to a small boy.

A lantern hung in the rear porch entrance at George Brown's as I passed the town line into Ledyard, but it was at the last turn in the road that our light shining through the darkness gave me my second wind, even though nearly a quarter of a mile, all uphill, remained. In spite of the rough roadway, I believe that my steps were longer than when the seven-mile hike lay before me.

Only when I reached the south pasture barway did the old house come into view. Silhouetted against that winter sky, its light beaming through the window as a beacon, it suddenly dawned on me that I was home. Seventeen hours and 45 minutes had passed since leaving the Seaman Gunner School, but the tedious waiting and the long hike in the snow were all worth the effort.

Passing through the gate, I saw tracks in the snow to and from the barn which told me that my father had completed his chores and was no doubt having breakfast. The door wasn't locked, and I needed but to turn the knob in order to enter. A glowing fire in the kitchen and a bubbling coffee pot greeted me.

But the most unforgettable welcome of all was my father, seated at the table under the glow of our ceiling hanging lamp. The soft, tender light in his eyes and the radiance of his smile told something far more than could ever be expressed. In his expression I read the words, "Welcome home, son." ✶

The Christmas Card I'll Never Forget

Continued from Page 110

that Marines Christmas card of 1943 could have reached a larger audience; that it hadn't been confined to families and friends of the 1st Marine Division.

Several years after the close of World War II, I decided to preserve the picture from my card by having it framed. It was then that I noticed, in very fine print on the back of the card, the crediting notation of the design to a technical sergeant of the Marine Corps.

I began wondering about this man whose creative work had moved me so eloquently. Had he, like my brother, been one of the fortunate Marines to come back? What had been his feelings and emotions when he had designed the card? If he had returned, would it be possible to locate him to ask these questions?

Through the cooperation of the Historical Branch of the USMC in Washington, D.C., I was able to reach the former technical sergeant artist. In a gracious reply to my query he wrote, "The idea I intended to show was the forces of peace-loving men tiredly moving out of the dark depth of a troubled, struggling world toward the inevitable peace symbolized by the age-old star of Bethlehem."

True, there has been no "World War" in the last five decades, but neither has there been worldwide peace. Will the pen (or man's words) never become mightier than the sword (or the bomb)?

As another Yuletide approaches a still-turbulent world, surely there can be no more appropriate prayer in our hearts than the greeting inscribed on that Christmas card I received so many years ago. "Peace on earth, good will toward men." ✶

School Yuletide

"Where is he that is born King of the Jews? For we have seen his star in the east, and are come to worship him." Those were the only words I had to memorize for the school's Christmas pageant. Twenty-five simple words from the Gospel according to Saint Matthew.

All I had to do was lead the three kings of the east up to "Herod" and say those 25 words. Then it was off to the manger with gold, frankincense and myrrh—our gifts for the newborn King.

I knew how important it was to get it right—Mrs. Simmons, my third-grade teacher (the director) had emphasized that to all of us elementary students who were saddled with speaking parts. All of our parents would be there, along with a lot of important people—like school board members and county officials.

Just 25 simple words. I could do that.

"Where is he that is born King of the Jews?" I queried Mama over the dinner dishes(she washed, I dried).

"Wha…? Oh, your lines for the pageant," Mama said. She always was pretty quick on such things.

"…for we saw his star in the east…"

"You mean, 'for we *have seen* his star in the east.' " She also was pretty quick to catch and correct a 9-year-old's mistakes.

"Oh, *shoot*…for we have seen his star in the

east, and are come to worship him." Mama smiled and nodded. Dishes were clean and so was my delivery.

The next few days were spent addressing every critter on the farm, every fence post, every person who dared show his or her face with the same query: "Where is he that is born King of the Jews?…" By Friday, the last day of school before Christmas break, I had the lines down perfectly.

The night of the pageant was suddenly upon us. The event was scheduled for the local nondenominational church—which at least had a small raised platform to serve as a stage. In the adjacent Sunday School rooms a bunch of nervous kids gathered to put on primitive costumes and make final preparations. "Where is he that is born King of the Jews?" I asked "Joseph," a fourth-grader. "Shut up!" was his only response.

Finally we were ready. The Christ Child was in the manger, surrounded by angels and shepherds. We three kings came to Herod and I intoned my lines. All the week's fretting—and it was over in a matter of a few seconds.

What was *not* over in a few seconds, however, was the memory. And that memory and many more like it were what made Christmas in schools back then so special. I hope you enjoy these stories of schooltime Yuletide from the Good Old Days.

—*Ken Tate, Editor*

Christmas in East Texas

By Vernon Marie Schuder

Christmastime in East Texas was wonderful! In the country schools we had real candles on a real tree, and it's a wonder we didn't burn down every schoolhouse in East Texas.

How well I remember the Christmas of 1920! I was 4 years old, in the first grade, and thought I was as big as anybody.

At the Christmas celebration I was sitting on a bench by P.J. He was a big boy in the second grade. My mother was the teacher. P.J. had been in the first grade for several years when we moved to this community. Mama kept him there a year and then promoted him to the second grade. P.J. thought Mama was wonderful. He said if "Miss Effie" hadn't come to Pine Prairie to teach he never would have gotten out of the first grade.

At this particular program, all the parents were there but P.J.'s father. He had told his children that he had to go to Huntsville on business, but would be back in time for the program if he could.

After the speeches and songs, Mama lit all the beautiful candles. They were fastened to the tree by little tin clips. She announced that Santa Claus himself was going to pay us a visit! He was going to give out the presents! We were properly thrilled and tried to be real good.

You didn't see Santa Claus on every corner for weeks before Christmas in those days. After a jangle of sleigh bells (they sounded a lot like cowbells) in came Santa Claus.

Christmas

Santa himself was going to pay us a visit. We were properly thrilled and tried to be real good.

He began to give out the gifts. Pretty soon he backed up against the tree and the cotton trimming on his coat caught fire. Santa said some excited words entirely unsuited to dear old Santa. He ran from the building in flames.

All the fathers rushed out. They caught him, rolled him on the ground and put out the fire. He wasn't hurt, Mama said.

We children were still sitting inside on the benches. We were wailing, "Santa Claus is dead!" in heartbroken sobs. One man said Santa Claus was going back to the North Pole so Mrs. Claus could mend his suit.

Mama gave out the rest of the presents herself. As we happily munched away at the

We were wailing, "Santa Claus is dead!" in heartbroken sobs.

Christmas candy, P.J. whispered to me, "You know, when old Santy caught fire, and started cussin', he sounded jest like Papa does when he gets mad!" ✷

Charles Berger

The Christmas Dress

By Bernadette Dotto

Actions motivated by love are so special that they are never forgotten. We cherish these memories for as long as we live.

Such was the Christmas of 1941 when I was 11. At our one-room school, we always started preparing for our Christmas program two months before the holiday. There was a lot of excitement that afternoon when the teacher gave each of us our parts. Once again, I was given a leading role in the main play. That, of course, meant a lot of memorizing and practicing. To top it off, I was asked to sing a solo. I was shocked! I had never sung by myself before an audience. I was excited though somewhat scared. My solo was *The Blue Velvet Band* composed by Hank Snow. It had 12 verses, but I had learned it the previous summer. I had practiced it day in and day out, until I had memorized every word.

During the days that followed, the girls at school were talking about the new dresses they would wear on that special day. As for me, I was poring over the mail order catalog and drooling over the gorgeous outfits on display.

But I would not be buying from the catalog, since my older sister was a fantastic seamstress who could copy a dress even without a pattern just

My best friend had shown me, in the catalog, the outfit her mother had ordered for her. As for me, I had to perform before a village audience in my ugly pink plaid dress.

by looking at the picture in the catalog. One day I asked her if she would make a dress for me for Christmas. There was one in the catalog that I really liked. But she declined as she had no fabric. I was heartbroken, but I approached my mother about it. For some reason—one I don't recall—a new dress for me for Christmas was out of the question.

My mother politely reminded me that I had a new plaid dress, made for me in the fall, and it should be good enough for the school program. I went upstairs to my room feeling very disappointed. I couldn't believe that I would have to wear that dress for my big day. That dress— made of pink plaid—made me look like a 5-year-old kid. I was to sing a solo and I felt very grown-up; a new dress would give me so much more self-confidence.

Time just flew by as I was so busy with my studies and with rehearsing the Christmas program. In spite of everything, I still hoped to get a new dress.

In my mother's bedroom there was a trunk with a curved lid. I was always attracted to it because it contained all kinds of neat treasures. Every chance I had, when she was not around, I would slip into her bedroom and look inside the trunk.

On one occasion, as I was rummaging in that trunk, I found a beautiful blue dress. It was exquisitely made and the fabric felt soft and satiny under my fingers. I spread it out on the bed. I knew it wouldn't fit me as it was made for an adult. While I was admiring it, Mum walked in. "Oh, Mum!" I said. "How I would love to have a beautiful blue dress like this for the Christmas program."

She sat on the bed and looked at me with moist eyes. Mum explained to me how special that dress was to her. She had worn it once only—on her wedding day! She lovingly folded it and placed it back in the trunk.

Gently, my mother asked me not to rummage in her old trunk any more or she would lock it.

My mum was special! She was actually my adoptive mother. She never had children of her own. When she married my adoptive father, he was a widower with seven children! Then they adopted me at 17 months, after my own father drowned. They raised me and loved me as their own. I was too young then to appreciate her—as she deserved—but as I grew up, I realized what a great lady she was.

Meanwhile Christmas was getting closer. Excitement mounted as the day of the program approached. The whole village would attend. The boys went into the woods to cut fir branches and the girls made garlands to decorate around windows and blackboards. We hung up big red bows in the corners. Everything was so pretty.

Two days before the big day, we were all ready. As I walked home that late afternoon it was snowing. Big, fluffy, white flakes were softly floating around me. That, in itself, should have made me jump for joy.

But I could not shake off the sadness I felt. My best friend had shown me, in the catalog, the outfit her mother had ordered for her. This outfit had now been received and admired. It was a red plaid pleated skirt complete with white blouse and a red bow to close the frilly collar. How pretty it all looked!

As for me, I had to perform before a village audience in my ugly pink plaid dress. I could have cried!

Walking into my home, I noticed that Mum and my sister had mischievous smiles on their faces. I pretended not to notice, but right after supper I inquired what the big secret was about. Mum said "Oh! We have a little surprise for you, but first we do the dishes." Once the dishes were done and put away, my sister took me by the hand, asked me to close my eyes, and carefully led me upstairs with Mum close behind.

We entered my sister's bedroom. I was told to open my eyes and suddenly my eyes sparkled. Spread out on her bed was the most beautiful blue dress I had ever seen. I was ecstatic! With long puffy sleeves, this dress had a white collar trimmed with lace!

Merry Christmas

I was literally beaming with the love, joy and peace that only Christmas can bring.

Excitedly, my sister asked me to try it on to see how well it fit. Wasting no time, I soon had it on and—what joy!—it fit me perfectly. I felt the satiny fabric and realized it was familiar.

Looking at Mum, I said, "Mum you didn't—" But she cut me off, saying, "It's OK. I really had been looking for an excuse to put it to good use."

Yes, that lovely sister of mine had taken Mum's treasured wedding dress apart, piece by piece, and had redesigned it to fit her little 11-year-old sister.

Mine was a proud performance that evening in the Christmas program, as I happily displayed that beautiful blue dress, literally beaming with the love, joy and peace that only a Christmas season can bring to us all. Our family enjoyed many wonderful Christmas seasons, but this Christmas was one that I really cherished. It has remained in my memory for all these many years. ✶

Silver Moon Christmas

By Wilma Hawes Connely
As told to Connie Connely

D o you think one of us is in trouble?" I asked.

I could see my brother Doyle's frosty breath as he answered, "No, Mrs. Heckmaster smiled when she gave it to me." Doyle pulled the sealed envelope out of his coat pocket. "We'd better not worry about it and just give it to Mama like our teacher said."

Our boots crunched in the snow as my two younger sisters and I followed Doyle home from school.

"Put your gloves on, Bonnie! And, Velma, you should have your coat buttoned up!"

"Yes, Miss Bossy Wilma!" my sisters said in unison.

I frowned, then smiled and said, "Oh! I know what that note is about. It must be about our school's Christmas pageant coming up."

The four of us went to a one-room country school called Silver Moon. Doyle was the oldest in school, an eighth-grader. Bonnie was our youngest in school, a second-grader. Our youngest sister, Phyllis, was 4 years old.

Mrs. Heckmaster always acted friendly to our family. Mama and Daddy felt privileged when asked to help with school projects. Mrs. Heckmaster seemed especially proud of our oldest brother, Walter. After leaving Silver Moon, Walter had gone on to high school in town and had graduated as valedictorian. Shortly after graduation, Walter joined the Army; then World War II started.

"I hope the note is good news," Bonnie said.

"Yeah," Velma agreed. "Mama cries easily since we found out that Walter is missing in action."

"Who's Hitler and where's Europe?" Bonnie asked.

"Hitler is a mean man. And Walter is a long way from Neosho, Mo.," Doyle answered sadly.

"It's Santa Claus!" some of our classmates cheered.

Once home, we girls huddled around the potbellied stove to warm ourselves. Doyle handed the envelope to Mama. She read the note and smiled.

"What's it say?" I asked, glad to see her happy. She hadn't been feeling well, even before we'd received the news about Walter.

"Oh, Mrs. Heckmaster just wants me to help her do something," Mama said.

The next few days, Mama and Daddy laughed and whispered a lot. "Walter would want us to have a good Christmas," Daddy said one evening, cracking pecans. "Don't you kids worry! Your big brother is smart; he'll get found!" Daddy winked and added, "You know the good Lord is looking after him."

The night of the Christmas pageant, my sisters and I primped in front of the mirror. We wore our Sunday school dresses and Doyle slicked down his hair.

"This is a good-looking bunch!" Mama said, as she helped Phyllis put on her coat.

"Where's Daddy?" I asked.

"He'll be along later, Wilma. Don't worry about him," Mama said, hurrying us out the door.

During the program I kept watching for Daddy to come in and sit by Mama and Phyllis. After we sang *Jingle Bells* we heard, "Ho-ho-ho! Merry Christmas!"

"It's Santa Claus!" some of our classmates cheered.

My sisters and I giggled and Doyle grinned.

Santa Claus looked very familiar. He was our daddy! Now we knew what the note said. We knew our parents' secret.

I still can see Mama's proud face watching Daddy pass out the presents. He really hammed it up with his loud *Ho-ho-hos*.

At the end of the program, we held hands and sang *Silent Night*. I knew Mama was

We held hands and sang Silent Night.

thinking about Walter, because I could see tears in her eyes.

Mrs. Heckmaster probably didn't realize it, but her note that cold December day brought a few days of happiness into our home. It lifted my parents' spirits, giving them something to feel glad about. And I learned a lesson to last my whole life: I could be happy despite unhappy circumstances.

A few months later, Walter did "get found" and eventually made it safely back from World War II. Unfortunately, it was our mother's last Christmas with us because she died in the state tuberculosis sanitarium the following year.

My father lived to be 72 and my brothers and sisters now each live in different states. But in my Christmas memory, we're all young again, holding hands and singing Christmas carols in Silver Moon School. ✶

Gladys' Doll

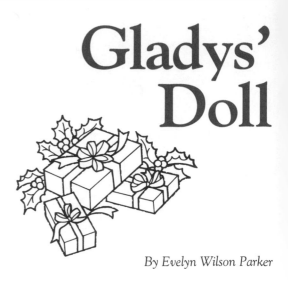

By Evelyn Wilson Parker

When Gladys Barnett thinks of her childhood, she remembers the good times she had with her family in Finney County, Kan.

Born in 1899, she was the next-to-youngest child of the large Foushee family.

There were 10 brothers and sisters altogether, spaced almost exactly two years apart. Today only she and her youngest sister, Anice, remain, and they still enjoy sitting down together to reminisce about their young lives. One memory that has endured throughout her life is perhaps not the happiest, but is filled with the lessons of reality.

The Foushee children rode horseback or traveled by horse and buggy to attend school at the little one-room schoolhouse about two miles away.

Each student looked forward to the annual Christmas party held at the school, and the year that Gladys was 8 was no exception. She had put particular effort into being good all that year, because Santa was going to come to the party, and her heart's desire was for him to bring her a doll.

"I remember the schoolhouse had been decorated for the party. They had found a dead tree [no one on the sparsely wooded plains would have thought to cut a precious live one], and they grandly decorated it with cotton and strings of cranberries and popcorn."

They had even put candles on the branches and lit them. "I don't know how they kept it from catching on fire, but it didn't!" She pauses for a moment, reflecting on the long-ago scene.

"In came Santa with a large bag. He laughed a hearty 'Ho, ho, ho!' and said he had dolls and toys for all the 'good girls and boys.' Well, I knew I'd been good, so had no doubt that I would get my doll!"

"In came Santa with a large bag. He laughed a hearty 'Ho, ho, ho!' and said he had dolls and toys for all the 'good girls and boys.' I knew I'd been good, so had no doubt that I would get my doll!"

As the dolls were drawn from the sack one by one and other girls' names were called, she patiently waited. But then the sack was empty except for some small bags that held candy, with maybe an orange or apple. One of those small bags was her gift, and she was crushed!

She cried all the way home, because she could not understand why Santa did not know she had been good. She did not learn until years later that the parents bought the gifts for their own children, and her folks—with 10 child-

ren—could not afford individual gifts that year.

All of the Foushee children received the same little bags, but none was so disappointed as 8-year-old Gladys.

"The next year, when I was 9, my name was called and I got my beautiful doll!" says Gladys. "But I knew in my heart I hadn't been any better that year, and probably not quite as good. Still, I was grateful for my doll."

She clearly remembers every detail of the exquisite china face. "She had eyes that opened and shut, real hair, and a leather body with joints that actually moved! I treasured my baby doll and cared for her so lovingly that I hardly ever took her out of the box she came in. In fact, I used to carry her around in my arms inside the box to keep her from getting hurt."

> ## "I treasured my baby doll and cared for her lovingly. I used to carry her around in my arms inside the box to keep her from getting hurt."

Once while Gladys was away from home, her oldest sister—then married—returned to visit with her little daughter.

Mr. and Mrs. Foushee allowed the youngster to play with Gladys' doll; she dropped it and the beautiful face was shattered.

It is still hard for her to think about this loss, and she has never understood why her parents allowed the irresponsible child to handle her doll. But they did, and the doll's head was broken, along with Gladys' heart.

"Oh, they gave me a new doll's head the next year, but this one was far inferior. The eyes did not blink, the hair was painted on, and—well, it just never meant the same to me."

While gladly sharing the memories she has of her childhood, Gladys does not dwell on the past. She enjoys life as it is today, and concentrates on a positive attitude about the future.

At age 95, she anticipates reaching the year 2000, and achieving the rare distinction of having lived in three separate centuries. There are very few who can attest to that, even those who might live well beyond 100. Still, she doesn't consider herself "old."

She lives alone, prepares her own meals, cleans her own home, attends church, crochets beautiful doilies and plays a mean game of Spite and Malice. One of her delicious pies is usually served when visitors come by.

Many are younger—say 80 or 85—and sometimes the conversation will find the guest commenting on an ailment, or the various aches and pains of age. Gladys usually will nod her head in sympathy, then respond softly, "Yes, I guess I'll have those problems too … when I get old." ✶

Secrets

By Russell Ford

ussell, why didn't you tell me you had drawn your name? I told all of you that you shouldn't have your own name." My heart sank into my shoes.

Since my first day at school I'd wished for December to hurry. My sister and brothers had always had such fun with their school Christmas program and exchange of gifts.

The previous December (1925) I was told "my time" would come—in two years. However, my parents arranged for me to enter the first grade a year early. Now I, a shy boy, small for my age, wanted to just fade away.

When Miss Harvey, my teacher, had passed the basket with our names I heard her say, "Don't tell." When I drew my name it was my secret, but I told Charles, my buddy. He blabbed. Cringing, I could hear one of Pa's sayings echoing in my ears. "A secret's no secret once you tell one other."

Slumping in my seat, I could barely hear Miss Harvey. "Russell has his own name and must trade. Anyone who would like to trade come to my desk." Several children left their seats.

"Russell," Mother said, "inside that package you've been eyeballing all week is that truck you wanted." Even today I see the wrapper, green holly leaves dotted with red berries.

Immobile, I sat remembering the previous Saturday. Mother had let me accompany her to downtown Birmingham. It was a high adventure. Three times the trolley we were riding was blocked by trains, their locomotives breathing steam and belching clouds of smoke. Once downtown, we entered F.W. Woolworth's five-and-dime. On a counter heaped with toys I saw a truck. A Mack. It had a chain drive just like the ones I'd seen when they built the turnpike through our village.

It was my secret, but I told Charles, my buddy. He blabbed. Cringing, I could hear one of Pa's sayings echoing in my ears. "A secret's no secret once you tell one other."

"Mama, do you suppose Santa could bring me a truck like that?"

Mother merely shrugged and led me to the lunch counter, helped me onto a stool, ordered a hot dog and a grape Nehi, then asked the pretty waitress, "Would you keep an eye on the boy?"

Mother moved away. I tried to keep track of her by watching the mirror back of the lunch counter, and I did not see her go near the toy counter. However, I did see a clerk walking down an aisle holding a truck. As I slurped the last drops of my Nehi, Mother appeared behind me with a shopping bag filled with gifts and said, "Let's go home."

I was awakened from my reverie by Miss Harvey rapping sharply on her desk. "Russell, can't you hear? Come, now!"

This time I drew Vera's name—the same Vera who always tried to slip in next to me when we lined up or played games.

I dragged home that afternoon, Thursday, Dec. 16, 1926. Tomorrow we'd exchange gifts, and I pondered, "What can I tell Mama?"

Stepping onto our front porch I sensed the door opening. I looked and saw Mama standing there. I blurted, "She made me— made me, Mama. Miss Harvey made me change names." My voice, colored by tears, cracked as I tried to explain what had happened.

"Russell," Mother said,

"inside that package you've been eyeballing all week is that truck you wanted. Soon's Pa gets home and has supper, he'll have to go swap it for something fittin' for a girl."

After supper, Pa reached for my package. Even today I see the wrapper, green holly leaves dotted with red berries. He said, "Maybe I'll make it 'fore the store closes." I stood on the sidewalk in front of our house and watched Pa trudge to the car stop. It seemed the trolley would never come.

It was late, but I could not sleep. Lying in bed I heard the front door open and Pa's voice tell Mama, "Never saw so many trains. Woolworth was closed." Their voices faded and I heard no more.

Friday morning the package was again lying on the buffet. The green holly leaves and red berries covering the package seemed to mock me. The tag had only read "Russell." "From" had been added in front of "Russell," and above that "To Vera." I told Mother I was sick, but she made me dress and I was off to school.

Our program over and the gifts distributed, I dared not glance toward Vera. I thought, *That truck by all rights should be mine.*

Miss Harvey stopped by my desk. I tried to sound excited. "Look, Miss Harvey, a sack of marbles." I held up a mesh sack with its 10 marbles. "See, there's a cat's-eye in there. I'll be using that for my taw."

I felt lips brushing my cheek, then heard Vera's whisper, "Gee, Russell, how did you know what I wanted most? It was a secret, and I didn't tell anyone. Not even my best friend. What a precious rubber dolly you gave me."

Christmas morning I found my truck under the tree. ✶

Tomorrow we'd exchange gifts, and I pondered, "What can I tell Mama?"

The Christmas Gift

By Molly Bien

My third grade teacher at P.S. 62 in Brooklyn had all the attributes a primary school teacher should have. She was kind, patient and soft-voiced.

She was also blond, slim and pretty. I liked her very much. My mother did also, as did my father, for yet another reason.

Her surname was Goodfleisch, which in German means "good meat." My father was a "kosher" Jewish butcher.

A few days before Christmas several of the children brought in their Christmas gifts for the teacher. Two other girls who sat near me placed theirs on their desks. I was entranced by the packaging—colorful wrapping with designs of Santa Clauses, pine trees and ornaments, each package bearing a crown of gleaming satin ribbons. They looked so beautiful, I just had to know what they contained.

One of the girls said her gift was a box of handkerchiefs. The other girl said her gift was a bottle of toilet water. Later, at recess on the school playground, several of the other children talked about their gifts for the teacher— a scarf, a string of beads, a key ring.

I thought of all these gifts as I left school for home, especially the two beautifully wrapped ones, which seemed to dance before my eyes, causing me to skip all the way. At supper that evening, I asked my parents if I could give Mrs. Goodfleisch a Christmas present. I asked hesitatingly since I knew money was scarce at our house. It was the Depression.

My father responded, "Yes," which I was very happy to hear. What he said next removed some of the luster:

"You may give her a chicken."

I was taken aback by this pronouncement, shocked that he would even consider this a suitable gift for her. None of the gifts the other children were giving even faintly resembled a chicken.

"I don't want to give her a chicken," I told my father. "I want to give her something pretty, in a box, something wrapped in tissue and pretty

> *I was entranced by the packaging— colorful wrapping with designs of Santa Clauses, pine trees and ornaments, each package bearing a crown of gleaming satin ribbons.*

wrapping paper, like a box of handkerchiefs or a scarf."

I didn't mention the toilet water, thinking he might question why toilet water is preferable to a chicken. He'd probably never experienced the floral scents in Woolworth's sample bottles.

"You can't wrap a chicken in pretty paper and ribbons," I said to him. "Besides a chicken doesn't smell nice. If you want to give her a chicken, then you or Mama give it to her. I won't. I would be too ashamed."

"Don't worry, she will like a chicken," my father said.

He was firm. Like many other immigrants, he was beset with economic problems. He was also relatively unsophisticated, and couldn't understand why I would want to give a gift to her which he considered frivolous.

My father's training as a kosher butcher hardly prepared him to share my enthusiasm for this Yuletide ritual.

A small sign in the bottom of his storefront window confirmed his products were strictly kosher, and under the supervision of the Rabbinical Council of New York.

My father may have thought he would be "excommunicated" by the synagogue if news of a Christmas gift leaving his home were to reach the congregation.

However, he may have felt a chicken, a kosher chicken at that, might add a little Chanukah to the Christmas, making the whole idea more palatable.

The following morning my mother accompanied me to school, carrying a brown paper butcher bag under her arm with a stewing

chicken inside. I was so embarrassed. I didn't want to go into the classroom, but she gently coaxed me to walk in with her.

My mother gave Mrs. Goodfleisch the chicken, wishing her a "Merry Christmas," adding, "This is a gift from Molly." I was barely able to look at Mrs. Goodfleisch as I, too, wished her a "Merry Christmas," the words barely able to leave my mouth.

Mrs. Goodfleisch accepted the chicken. She peered into the brown butcher bag. I squirmed.

"What a wonderful Christmas present!" she exclaimed, her face crinkling up into a wide smile as she thanked my mother and me. "This will make a lovely Christmas dinner."

I was flabbergasted! So elated, I floated to my seat. She wouldn't receive another gift like this one. The chicken was probably her first, and more than likely her last, "kosher" Christmas gift. ✶

No Santa Claus? Oh, No!

By Barba Covington McCarty

The magic of Santa at Christmas is something that every child who is permitted to believe in Santa never forgets.

The wonderment of Santa coming to your house in the middle of the night, drinking milk and eating cookies, leaving presents for everyone and never waking anyone, is enough to stir a child's imagination from year to year.

As a child, I imagined that Santa tiptoed in the front door (we had no chimney), peeked into where we were sleeping, sat down and ate the cookies and drank the milk, then returned to the front porch for the gifts he would leave us.

We left banana pudding for Santa one year and I thought he might not like it. My father, who loved banana pudding, assured me that Santa would like it, too.

I wondered how Santa kept all the gifts separated. He always knew which presents were mine and which ones were for my little sister, Beverly, who was 15 months younger than I was.

Every year on the day after Santa came, I looked for reindeer tracks. I could not understand why a dog left tracks in the dirt and a whole bunch of reindeer didn't. Of course, any questions concerning reindeer tracks were answered by the fact that the reindeer had been on the roof. So, I imagined that Santa jumped off the roof with a big bag of our gifts.

I found out there was no

Santa right before Christmas holiday vacation was to begin while eating the traditional Christmas lunch with other first-grade students at Graham School.

That holiday meal was the first of many just like it that would be served to me at Christmas every year in school cafeterias. The menu never varied from chicken and dressing, green beans, mashed potatoes, a roll and milk. Some cranberry sauce was on the side of the plate and dessert was a plain white sheet cake with butter frosting.

Just as I was seated with my food tray and was moving over to let another girl sit on the lunch bench, Jimmy Newsom, who was sitting in front of me, announced, "There's really not a Santa Claus, it's your mother and daddy who put stuff under the Christmas tree."

Some of the kids argued with him, but he turned to a bigger student sitting at the table behind him and said, "Tell them who Santa Claus is." The older boy laughed and said, "Your mama and daddy."

That settled it. Jimmy was right. He explained further that my mother and daddy bought the gifts and hid them until Christmas night, and they put them under the tree while we were asleep. "Then," he said, "they sit down and eat the cookies and drink the milk."

I said nothing but I was very disappointed because I really wanted there to be a Santa Claus.

I went home after school and started looking for a place big enough to hide Christmas gifts. I told no one what I was doing or

As a child, I imagined that Santa tiptoed in the front door (we had no chimney), peeked into where we were sleeping, ate the cookies and milk, then brought the gifts he would leave us.

that Jimmy had told the lunch crowd that there was no Santa Claus. I kept searching and searching.

The first place I looked was in a large quilt box that Mama had in the back bedroom. The box was large enough for Bev and me both to get into at the same time, and we had a few times. There was nothing inside except the quilts.

Every year on the day after Santa came, I looked for reindeer tracks.

I searched under beds and behind furniture and in all the closets. In the top of one of the closets, I discovered a door that I had never noticed. The door led to the attic.

As soon as it was safe for me to look in the door, I got a tall stool and stood it on a chair and looked in that door. Just as I was about to get a peek at what I thought could be dolls in boxes, Mama came in and made me get off the stool and chair.

I looked up there again later and the boxes were gone.

My search for Santa's gifts was on again. I would not believe there was no Santa unless I found those hidden treasures of Christmas. School was out for the holidays and I had a lot of searching time.

Early one morning, I found them. There were two dolls in their original boxes inside the big quilt box under the quilts. I sure hoped that the red-haired doll with the curly hair was mine.

There were also two cancans, just alike, as most of our things were. We wanted cancans to make our dresses stand out and make that rustling sound that cancans make.

I knew why Jimmy Newsom had told the whole class. I could not keep this secret either. It was the biggest secret I had ever known. Later that day, I told Beverly there was no Santa Claus. She pouted at me and said, "Yes, there is."

I informed her that Mama and Daddy bought our presents and hid them until Christmas night.

"Huh uh!" she screamed at me. She insisted that there was a Santa Claus. So I told her, "I'll show you our dolls."

She said "No," but the temptation of seeing her Christmas doll was too big for her.

We tiptoed into the back room, and I raised the lid of the quilt box very slowly. Bev was peering over into that quilt box like she thought we had found a gold mine. She grimaced as I lifted the heavy quilts up so she could see the doll boxes.

Then, she started crying. I had no idea what to do then. I knew if she cried we were going to get caught. I tried to put my hand over her mouth which made her cry more. The thought of getting caught did not quiet her crying.

My search for Santa's gifts was on again. I would not believe there was no Santa unless I found those hidden treasures of Christmas.

She took off running to Mama who thought something was wrong with her.

I stayed in the next room and waited and listened. Beverly told Mama, "Barba storied to me; she said there ain't no Santy Claus."

Mama quieted her crying and I ran outside to get away from the whole mess Jimmy Newsom had started and I had finished.

Mama called me in the house and talked to both of us about the matter of Santa Claus. Afterward, I got in trouble for showing Bev the Christmas dolls and cancans and for looking myself.

The next day we looked in the box; the dolls and cancans were gone again. I didn't have the nerve to check the top of the closet again. I was afraid I would get caught and I was already in enough trouble too close to Christmas.

The next time Beverly and I saw the dolls and cancans was under the Christmas tree on Christmas morning. The cancans scratched us too much to wear them. The red-haired doll with the curly hair was mine. I named her Linda.

I bet Santa sneaked her in the front door while I was asleep. ✶

The White Tennis Slippers

By Mrs. LaGrone Williams

Christmas pageants are always a highlight in a child's life, and this one in the year of 1929 was just that for me. What a thrill it was to be an angel with a flowing white cheesecloth costume, shimmering tinsel wings attached to the back, and the tinsel halo perched precariously on my head.

As we all gathered together with our teachers to talk about the costumes needed for the pageant, the question arose as to the type of shoes the angels would wear, and one teacher suggested white tennis slippers.

When I heard them say "white tennis slippers," I was overjoyed. To understand this joy over something as commonplace now as tennis

What a thrill it was to be an angel with a flowing white costume, shimmering wings and tinsel halo.

The night of the pageant arrived with all the excitement of an opening night. Now it was time for the angels to march down to view the Baby Jesus.

shoes, one would need to know that this was the beginning year of the Great Depression, and just to keep a large family in plain sturdy shoes was a problem. In my secret heart I had longed for white tennis slippers, and I had asked many times for them, but my mother would always tell me that we had to do without these because they were not a necessity. When I heard the talk of tennis slippers, I realized that here was my chance to have my heart's desire.

As the teachers talked over the tennis slipper idea, it was decided this was an added expense which most could not afford, and so the idea was dropped, but here is where the plot thickens. I was disappointed to learn that the tennis slipper idea was dropped, but instead of relaying this bit of information to my mother, I simply neglected to tell her because I wanted them so desperately.

Then the search for the tennis slippers began, with Mama grumbling all the time about my teachers requesting such a thing. In those days tennis slippers were not stocked year-round. We went from store to store, looking for them, and finally found one who had carried a few sizes over. The only size I could wear were really too short, but I drew up my toes to prove

to Mama they were fine. The purchase was made but Mama gave me one warning: I would have to wear the shoes that summer even if they were too short. I scarcely heard her, I was so pleased with my shoes.

The night of the pageant arrived with all the excitement of an opening night. Now it was time for the angels to march down to view the Baby Jesus. How angelic I felt! Down we went with our beautiful costumes. It was then that I looked down at my feet and realized that Mama would see that I alone had white tennis slippers. The enormity of what I had done rushed over me. My sins had found me out!

After the pageant, as we walked home through the beautiful, cold, star-filled Christmas Eve, I waited for the chastisement I knew would surely come, and come it did, in Mama's disappointment in me. All she said was, "Polly, you storied to me," but it cut me to the quick. Nothing more was said; nothing more needed to be said; I had learned my lesson.

True to Mama's promise, I did have to wear the white tennis slippers that summer, with their toes cut out to make room. A constant reminder, my white tennis slippers had lost their appeal. ✶

Unforgettable Christmas

By Ada Breise Cromer

Happy laughter drifted on the breeze on a sunny November day when my brother and I walked homeward from country school with our two best friends. They lived with their parents on a farm next to ours.

Amy and I were 11. Of equal height, we were both in our slender years. Similarities ended there. Blue-eyed Amy had honey-colored hair like her Swedish ancestors. Mine was the auburn of a ripe chestnut. Mark was 8, one year younger than my brother David. David was a quiet boy, but the fun-loving Mark gave him added zest and much laughter.

We four had shared a happy summer. We had run barefoot through the green pastures and waded in the warm shallow ponds in the woodland clearings of my father's farm. Agile as monkeys, we climbed among the limbs of the huge oak trees, stirring the blue jays to raucous cries and the squirrels to scolding chatter. Sunny hours were spent playing hide-and-seek and rolling with laughter in the tall grass of the hay meadow. We made a tire swing and spun 'round in it till we were dizzy. The tree house we built was a dream world high in the cool branches of an ancient maple.

How could we know that disaster lay ahead—an experience which threatened to ruin our usual joyful Christmas? On that particular November day we left the school-yard in a playful mood, not knowing it was our last day together.

Mark was a carefree fellow and as lively as a spring colt as we moseyed along the dirt road toward home. With his shoes scuffing the dust and a smile on his round face, he kept us laughing with amusing antics.

We four had shared a happy summer. How could we know that disaster lay ahead—an experience which threatened to ruin our usual joyful Christmas?

"Hope Mama baked bread today and maybe some cookies," he said, turning a somersault. Then, whistling, he skipped on ahead. He stopped suddenly, and taking an apple from his sweater pocket, he bit into it hurriedly to satisfy his hunger.

"I hate school," he said with a grimace. Teacher had kept him in his seat at noon and during the last recess because he'd kept everyone giggling with his comical facial expressions when she wasn't looking.

Watching him swallow the last morsel of apple, I said, "If teacher wouldn't let me eat my lunch, I wouldn't go to school."

"I'm not going tomorrow," he said, kicking an imaginary object and spinning around. "I'll hide and Mama won't find me." He flipped into a cartwheel and landed on his feet in swirling dust. He looked at us and grinned, and his eyes were twinkling again.

"Let's not go home yet," I said, leading the way to the edge of the road. Amy was carrying Mark's books. I had his lunch pail, and I set it beneath the nearby field fence. "Let's talk about Christmas," I suggested, seating myself on the grassy bank. "I'm wishing for some new ice skates."

"I wish I'd get a shiny new sled," Mark added.

"I know," said David. "Let's look for four-leaf clovers to wish with."

Amy rose quickly to her feet. "Mama said to hurry home, and Papa will scold us for being late with our chores."

We were nearing the driveway to their home, and looking toward the house I saw Amy's parents watching from the front yard. We had walked several paces before Mark paused and,

with round-eyed seriousness exclaimed, "We forgot my lunch pail."

His short legs carried him skipping across the road to get it, and then he was running back to join us. Amy paused at the road's edge to wait for him.

None of us saw or heard the speeding motorcycle as it topped the crest of a hill. In a matter of seconds it zoomed down the incline. Its sudden roar was followed by a terrifying impact. A great cloud of dust soared skyward, carrying with it lunch pails, books and flying papers.

Safe on the opposite side of the road, David and I stared in horrified silence. The dust slowly cleared to show Mark lying motionless in the center of the driveway entrance. Amy had been thrown into the ditch. Shocked by the sight, I screamed, "Amy and Mark! They've been hit!"

Their mother and father came running down the driveway, shouting to one another in Swedish. By then the cyclist had left his ditched motorcycle and was lifting Mark's limp body in his arms. Moments before, he'd been full of life. Now he lay pale and deathly still. Amy had struggled to an upright position and was staring silently about her with a dazed expression.

The doctors said he might never walk again. With this news, Teacher canceled plans for the Christmas program. Instead we began painting Christmas cards.

"Get a doctor! Get a doctor!" Mark's father cried brokenly. The mother knelt beside Amy, sobbing and twisting her apron with helpless frustration.

As David and I turned toward home, Mark's father shouted behind us. "Have your mama call two doctors. My boy is hurt bad!"

Later that night after my parents returned from the hospital, I told my mother between sobs, "It was all my fault. If we'd come straight home instead of playing along the road—if I'd gone back for it, not Mark …"

"Hush, you mustn't think that. You couldn't know. And you certainly meant no harm." She smoothed David's newly mended shirt and folded it with hands that trembled. She added softly, "He has good doctors. We can only hope and pray."

"What about Amy?" I asked.

"Her worst injury was a broken leg," she replied.

A stranger came to our farm home and questioned David and me. With bowed heads we stood silently beside our mother.

"They're so young," she said, holding our hands tightly as though she wanted us never to walk that road again.

Father said, "No judge in his right mind will let that man go without a stiff penalty. If I was on that jury …"

In mid-November, Amy and her parents moved away. Gone was the play and laughter as David and I went to and from school. After Thanksgiving the pupils began rehearsing for our Christmas program. Sad faces bent over books and papers, and voices recited in low monotone. Teacher shook her head and said, "We'll try it again tomorrow."

Three weeks before Christmas I received a letter from Amy which I shared with my schoolmates. Mark was still in the hospital, she wrote. He was swathed in casts and bandages. The doctors said he might never walk again.

With this news, Teacher canceled plans for the Christmas program. Instead we began painting Christmas cards, each with our own message. We decorated them with bits of tinsel and tiny red paper bells. The boys made tops and whistles and a small wooden train, sanded them all to satin smoothness and painted them with bright colors. Teacher brought a small tree and we trimmed it with chains of red and green paper rings, strings of colored beads and shiny ornaments donated by several parents.

Most exciting was the collection fund. Pennies, nickels and dimes tinkled inside an empty coffee can. David and I emptied our toy banks and then ran errands and did extra work so we could add to the collection. "It will buy a big gift," our teacher said. The coins mounted and soon dollar bills were added by neighboring fathers.

"We have $15," David told Mother. There was almost a lilt in his voice again. We children were seated at the dining room table while Mother read to us. It was a story abut a lame boy who couldn't walk without crutches. On Christmas Eve he feel asleep by the tree. Leaving his crutches where they lay, his father carried him to bed. The next morning, with his gaze fixed on the glitter and toys, the boy walked across the room to the Christmas tree.

"Christmas is a time for miracles," Mother told us when she finished the story. "Wonderful things often happen then."

I was home with a cold that last day before holiday vacation, so I missed the excitement at school. When David came home that afternoon, he had joyous news about a certain letter.

"Mark's father wrote it," he explained with eyes shining. "The cars and toys and tree and everything got to the hospital all the same day, and Mark is going home for Christmas. The doctor said he's going to be all right."

He paused for breath and then continued, "He's going to walk and play again. His father is going to use the collection money to buy a red sled and train and a cowboy suit."

"Merciful heavens!" Mother exclaimed, holding her hands high in the air. "All that. Lord be praised!"

I forgot my sore throat and miserable cold and shrieked with joy. David turned a somersault the way he'd seen Mark do and we all laughed until the little bells on the Christmas tree trembled and tinkled.

Although all this happened long ago, it was a Christmas I'll never forget. It was the year I learned about faith and hope, about parental love, and the delight that comes with the doing, and the pleasure in giving. Too, I learned of the blessing of miracles. ✶

It's more than "Merry Christmas"
that I am wishing you,
It's "Bright and Happy Every Day"
the coming twelve months through.

Christmas Greetings

John Slobodnik

Chapter Seven

Seasons Gone By

I love to sing. Just ask Janice about that. She'll tell you that it doesn't take much to get me going. It seems that just about anything will remind me of an old show tune, or a song from the radio when it was my principal nighttime entertainment.

I've wondered at times what caused me, at an early age, to love to sing and make music. I enjoyed many Saturday nights at get-togethers at one of my uncles' homes, where a bonfire or camp lantern lighted a circle of friends and family singing heartily. I was one of the loudest—if not exactly on key—at church services.

But it was Christmas—and a special uncle—that really sealed my devotion to the field of music.

Singing carols was always a major part of our Yuletide preparations. After trudging through snow into the hollow across the road from our home, selecting a cedar tree and cutting it down, our family group tugged and pulled it back to the house. There it was properly trimmed and mounted in the living room with the few ornaments we had and a lot of tinsel to fill in the gaps.

One Christmas, when I was about 9 or 10, that special uncle of mine stopped off as we were putting the finishing touches on the Christmas tree. B.H. is his name, and he is Daddy's youngest brother. (Once I asked Daddy how come B.H. had only letters for a name.

Daddy said, with tongue in cheek, that his father and mother had had so many children that, after a while, they quit giving them names and just started giving them letters: S.C., W.O. and B.H. I think B.H. stands for something, but I never knew what it was.)

Anyway, B.H. was over and brought his guitar, which was never far from where he was. He strummed and sang with us to strains of *Silent Night, O Come All Ye Faithful* and other seasonal favorites. B.H. was always my hero; he was talented, funny and interesting to be around. When I overheard him tell Mama that he thought I had a pretty good voice, it sealed in concrete my interest in singing and music.

If it had come from anybody else, it wouldn't have mattered. But B.H. thought I had a good voice, so it must be true. (Years later I would sing with B.H.'s country music band at my little sister's wedding reception. I thought I had "arrived.")

It's funny how thoughts of the Christmas season always take you back to some warmly glowing memory. Mine is of stoking that old wood stove until the living room was toasty, gathering around the tree and singing with my Uncle B.H.

I guess that's why those seasons gone by were the best from the era we call the Good Old Days.

—*Ken Tate, Editor*

The Christmas Turkey That Wasn't

By Charles B. O'Dooley

It all started one day when my sister Grace and I were spending the day with our Uncle Harry and Aunt Jane. Aunt Jane, in my opinion, was one of the best cooks who ever lived, and I always looked forward to spending the day at her place and getting to eat my fill of her cooking.

Grace and I would help Aunt Jane do small chores around the place. On that particular day we were helping her clean the turkey coop.

Uncle Harry usually raised 50 to 60 turkeys each year for market. At our ages—I was 5 and my sister was 7—we naturally had a thousand and one questions. "How do you raise turkeys?" "Were they borned that big?" And so on.

Aunt Jane was very patient with all our questions. She showed us an egg and explained that the mother turkey sat on the eggs for 25 days and then little baby turkeys would come out of the eggs.

When we got ready to go home with full stomachs and smiles of satisfaction on our faces, Aunt Jane gave us two turkey eggs and told us that if we would put them under a setting hen, we each would have our own little turkey to raise.

The next morning Pop placed the two eggs under an old setting hen and we sat back and waited for the young turkeys to appear. When you are only 5 or 7, 25 days can seem like a lifetime. Every day my sister and I would lift the old hen to see if our turkeys were there. By the end of three weeks, we were sure that the eggs had gotten cold and would not hatch.

On the morning of the 26th day, as we entered the chicken house, the old hen was down on the floor scratching in the straw, and right behind her were two balls of fluff, chirping and looking bewildered. As the days passed and they lost their fuzz and started getting feathers, I noticed the mother hen looking at them as if to say, "I never had any babies that looked like you two before!"

The two baby turkeys were hatched in mid-April, and by

the end of May you could tell that one was a tom turkey and one was a hen. We named them Tom and Alice.

Grace and I cleaned out an old, unused doghouse. We put fresh straw on the floor and moved the hen and two chicks into it. Tom grew like a weed, but Alice never seemed to get off the ground and start growing. Our dad told us that turkeys were hard to raise and caught many diseases, and that they were the dumbest bird there was. He said they would even lift their heads up with their mouths open in a rainstorm and drown themselves. I don't know if this is what happened, but one morning after a hard rain we found Alice lying on her back with both legs in the air.

> *Pop kept telling my sister and me that we would have Tom for Christmas dinner. This bit of news upset my sister and me to no end as we thought of Tom's fate.*

When Tom was about 3 months old he chased the old hen out of the doghouse and took it over for himself. He wouldn't associate with the flock of chickens we had, but would go off by himself to feed. He liked to go into the edge of the woods and scratch around rotten logs for grub worms.

The year was 1932 and there were still some chestnuts left that the blight hadn't got. In the fall of that year, Tom spent all his time under the chestnut trees eating his fill of the nuts. He grew to be a magnificent bird with a long beard and carried himself in a stately and imposing way.

Pop kept telling my sister and me that we would have Tom for Christmas dinner, but we never knew just what he meant until the first of December when Mom told him to pen Tom up and feed him nothing but corn so he would be nice and plump to butcher the day before Christmas. This bit of news upset my sister and me to no end, and we went about with long, sad faces as we thought of Tom's fate.

Pop told us that's what turkeys were raised for, to eat, and that next year we would raise a

whole bunch of them. But this didn't pacify us and we would go off by ourselves and talk about it.

One day Grace and I were sitting under Tom's favorite chestnut tree making plans to save Tom from the dinner table. Grace said, "You know, if Tom wasn't here on Christmas Eve, Mom couldn't butcher him."

I said, "What do you mean?"

"You know that small cave back in the woods?" she asked. "Why couldn't we hide Tom there till after Christmas?" So that's what we did.

We prepared for the abduction of Tom all that day. We got a piece of chicken wire for the mouth of the cave, and a sack of corn to take along and feed Tom. Late in the afternoon when Tom was feeding on the edge of the woods, we gathered him up and headed for the cave. He didn't seem to mind what we were doing, and seemed to know we were saving him. A small stream of water ran through the cave, so we didn't have to worry about him being thirsty.

We put him in the cave with an ample supply of corn and some chestnuts, and put the chicken wire across the front and piled brush over it. Anyone passing would have to look pretty hard to see there was a cave there at all.

Nobody missed him until the next evening when Mom asked if anyone had seen Tom. Finally they came to the conclusion that he must have wandered too far into the woods and a fox got him.

Every day after that, Grace and I would tell Mom we were going to look for Tom, and we would head for the cave where we would feed him and talk to him for awhile.

A week before Christmas there came a big snowstorm. Grace and I worried about Tom and how he would make it without us feeding him each day.

The storm held on and it was cold until after New Year's. On the first warm day, Grace and I headed for the cave to check on Tom. When we got there, the wire had been pushed aside and Tom was nowhere to be seen.

I started to cry. "An old fox found Tom and ate him up," I said.

Grace said, "No, he broke out himself. See how the wire is pushed out from the inside?"

We came to the conclusion that Tom had gotten so hungry that he went hunting for food and had probably joined a flock of wild turkeys and was all right. When we got back to the house, Mom could tell something was wrong and she asked us what it was. Finally we both broke down in tears and told her the whole story—how we had hid Tom in the cave to save him, and how each day we had gone to feed him.

Mom said, "So that's where you went each day when you said you were looking for him?"

"Yes, Ma'am," we said.

When the rest of the family heard about it they all laughed at the ingenuity and cleverness shown by a 7-year-old girl and a 5-year-old boy to save their pet bird. Pop said that in all probability, Tom had joined a flock of wild turkeys, and if he had, he would probably make it through the winter.

The cold winter months passed and we had all but forgotten Tom. Then one day early in April, when everything had turned green and the sun was shining and the birds were busy building their nests, Mom was in the yard getting her flower beds ready to plant. She straightened up to rest her back and looked up toward the woods, then called all of us to come quickly.

We all ran outside and looked where Mom was pointing. Lo and behold, there was Tom, and with him, a fine-looking hen turkey. You could tell that Tom had taken her for his bride by the way he was strutting and opening his tail feathers to form a fan as he walked around and around her.

Grace and I yelled, "Tom! Tom, you've come home!"

Tom looked at us and put his head next to the hen. I bet he was telling her to follow him. Tom led the way and the hen followed, and he made straight for the doghouse and went inside. The hen stayed out while Tom dug out all the old, wet straw. Grace and I quickly ran to the barn and got fresh straw for the honeymoon cottage.

After we put the straw in the doghouse, Tom stepped aside and let his bride enter. To make a long story short, Tom and his mate raised 12 young turkeys that year, and over the next five years raised dozens more.

One day when Tom didn't come back from the woods, we went looking for him and found him dead under his favorite tree. He had died of old age. Grace and I buried him by the side of the cave where he had found his bride. ✶

Christmas Is Love

By Josie Patrick

I was feverish that Christmas Eve the year I was 5 years old, or I should never have been put to bed on the couch in the living room.

It was an unfolding couch that made a nice double bed, reserved for Mama and whichever one of us children was ill. That was the only nice thing about being sick—getting to sleep with Mama.

I was awakened from my sleep when I heard Mama say, "Santa Claus, your suit fits you nicely."

I opened my eyes, and sure enough, there stood Santa Claus. That was a funny thing for Mama to say to Santa Claus. Here he was right here in the room with me and Mama, and I'd never liked to be near him. He frightened me.

I remembered last year he'd come in on Christmas morning and handed presents to us all—that is, all except Papa, who wasn't there. When Santa Claus called his name and left some packages for him, I'd asked, "Where's Papa, Mama?"

Mama had said, "Oh, he'll be here in a minute," but Papa didn't come till after Santa Claus left.

I remembered my sister Dora, who was two years older than I, kept looking hard at Santa Claus. When my brother Johnny tried to pull his beard, Santa Claus pushed his hand away and backed off.

I didn't even want to get close to him. He was funny looking, but I kept wanting him to go away and I kept wishing Papa would come.

Just like now. I wanted Santa Claus to go away, but I was afraid to say a word. Even the beauty of the Christmas tree with the lights glowing and the ornaments sparkling didn't dim my fear. I kept wishing Papa would come. If I told him to make Santa Claus go away, I knew he would.

We had all sat around the tree the night before. Mama held me in her lap while Papa told us a story about a bright star that some men watching their sheep followed. They kept going till they came to where Baby Jesus was.

After the story, Papa said, "Now all off to bed. Sissy needs to go to sleep and all of you'll be up early to see Santa Claus."

I started wishing then that Santa Claus wouldn't stay like he did last Christmas, that he would slip in and leave some presents and go away before we woke up. I went to sleep wishing that, and I'd awakened to see him right there in the room.

I wished Papa would come. I wouldn't be afraid then.

Mama surely didn't seem afraid of Santa Claus. She was standing right up close to him, and suddenly she reached up and tweaked his ear. Then she gave his beard a yank and pulled it right off.

Santa Claus had Papa's face.

"Honey," Mama said, "you make the best Santa Claus I've ever seen."

I wasn't afraid anymore. I knew Santa Claus was Papa. I knew he went with everything that made Christmas so wonderful.

Young as I was, I knew it wasn't the presents that Santa Claus brought that made Christmas a time of happiness.

It was what Mama and Papa gave us all year long.

It was LOVE. ✴

My Most Unusual Christmas

By Alma G. Keyser

I was 8 years old on that 1890 Christmas. It is the first Christmas that I really remember, so here goes:

My dear mother made a grab bag to help Old Santa. She would go out to the old wood house to get an old wooden barrel hoop, then to the old granary and get an old gunnysack, gather up some string and, with the aid of a homemade needle, sew the gunnysack to the hoop. The grab bag completed, Mother would pitch in to wrap oranges, apples, candies, little cakes, black walnuts, hickory nuts, chestnuts and a few small toys. Then to put humor in the occasion, she would wrap the turnips, potatoes, a small cabbage, onions, and pieces of coal. It would be lots of fun to see who got the cabbage head to joke about. My mother's expression was, "Two heads are better than one, even though one is a cabbage head."

My oldest brother, William Henry Hart, was the Santa Claus. He would come in the old dining room when the children got lined up around the room. Starting with my father and mother, then the children, each would reach in the old grab bag and come up with something. I was always last, being the youngest. The fun was not knowing what we would get.

Santa would go around until the grab bag was empty. Then we children would go to our stockings on the fireplace mantel and find something we needed and a gift. Mine was a little wooden washing set. It consisted of table with a little wringer, and a little tub with a washboard in it. I still have them and they have been played with. I prize them.

One great joy was to look at Montgomery Ward's catalog to see their toys and say, "I want this or that." Children in my very young life never saw toys, dolls and the like except right at Christmas, not all the year around. I really think there was much more joy getting a few things from our stockings and the surprises from the old grab bag. My dear father was blind but he enjoyed the grab bag with us. ✶

Those Wonderful Christmas Cookies

By Ginger K. Nelson

This feels like it's going to be really good to work with this year," my aunt says, squishing cookie dough through her fingers until the consistency feels right. I dip my finger in and taste. "Better than ever. I think I'd like a bit more of a lemony taste." My mother squeezes fresh lemon over the dough. "Perfect," I proclaim. We are ready to roll—literally.

Rolling pins, bags of flour, a pile of Christmas cookie cutters and several assorted baking tins line my kitchen table. My mother tends the oven, making sure each delectable cookie is baked just right. In her area of the kitchen, long sheets of waxed paper line the counters, filling rapidly with Santas, stars, sleighs and bells delicately brushed with egg white and sprinkled with colored sugar.

My aunt and I roll and cut, reminding my mother when "they smell done." This is one way that we carry on traditions from my Hungarian grandmother. Using a kitchen scale and her senses along with her good sense, Grandmother produced some wonderful-tasting cookies whose cinnamony and lemony fragrances remind me each year of her. Through the Christmas cookie baking, I can recall cuddling into her ample folds, gently feeling the softness of her carefully pulled-back white hair, and watching in awe as those hands swiftly, perfectly shaped each cookie.

> *My aunt and I roll and cut the cookies, reminding my mother when "they smell done." This is one way that we carry on traditions from my Hungarian grandmother.*

Now I watch my 83-year-old mother and my 79-year-old aunt deftly knead and roll cookie dough, reciting the same stories each year.

"Remember how Mama's cookies were always the same? And how she could roll them so thin without breaking them?" Each year I take pictures of our cookie-baking sessions to imprint these memories on my mind. And I wonder if someday my grandchildren will delight in helping me make those

wonderful Christmas cookies which will turn into memories each year during the holidays.

★★★

For all the following cookies set out ingredients until they reach room temperature so that they are easily mixed. Blend together by hand according to instructions in each recipe. Shape dough into large balls, cover with waxed paper, and refrigerate.

The chilling will enable you to roll out the dough with greater ease. Chilling time should be approximately one hour *or* until easy to handle.

When ready to begin, remove one ball of dough at a time, leaving the remainder in the refrigerator. Roll out according to specific instructions. Because most of the recipes require only the egg yolks, save the whites for the vanilla *kipfle* and refrigerate the remainder in a small container.

Use these extra egg whites as a topping for all but the vanilla *kipfle*. Beat the whites with a fork and brush lightly across the tops of the cookies before adding Christmas sprinkles. This makes a shiny surface and keeps the decorations from falling from the cookies.

All cookies are baked on ungreased cookie sheets. (The new insulated cookie sheets are best coated lightly with vegetable spray or as directions indicate.) After baking, set aside until completely cooled before removing to place in storage containers.

Thin Butter Cookies

½ pound sweet butter
2½ cups flour
Grated rind of ½ lemon
1½ cups confectioners' sugar
3 egg yolks

Mix all ingredients until smooth. Roll out on floured board, cut with desired cookie cutters. Decorate and bake in a 350-degree oven about 10 minutes, or until lightly browned. Makes 4 dozen cookies.

Linza Cookies

4¼ cups flour
1 cup margarine
2 cups sugar
Pinch of salt
2 whole eggs plus 1 egg yolk
1 teaspoon baking soda
Juice of 1 lemon

Mix flour, margarine, sugar and salt with hands. Make a well in middle and put in eggs, egg yolk, baking soda, and lemon juice.

Mix well. Roll on floured board to about ¼ inch in thickness. Shape with desired cookie cutters and decorate. Bake in a 350-degree oven for about 10 minutes, or until lightly browned. Makes 4 dozen cookies.

Cinnamon Cookies

4½ cups flour
1 pound sweet butter
1 cup confectioners' sugar
2 whole eggs
1 teaspoon baking powder
½ cup (or more) cinnamon

Mix all ingredients well. Roll out on floured board; cut with desired cookie cutters; decorate. Bake in a 350-degree oven about 10 minutes, or until done. Makes 5 dozen cookies.

Cream Cheese Cookies

½ pound cream cheese
1 cup confectioners' sugar
Grated peel from ½ lemon
½ teaspoon baking powder
½ pound sweet butter
1 egg yolk
2 cups flour
¼ teaspoon salt

Mix together, shape into balls, and refrigerate for *several hours*. Roll out about ½ inch thick on floured board. Bake at 350 degrees for about 20 minutes or until lightly browned. Makes 5 dozen cookies.

Vanilla Kipfle

A few days prior to baking, place a vanilla bean in each box of confectioners' sugar you will use to bake and to roll to give added flavor. Use 2–3 boxes. When ready to coat baked cookies, place some of the vanilla sugar in a large container. A roasting pan works well.

3½ cups flour
1 cup ground almonds
3 teaspoons vanilla
1¾ cups confectioners' sugar
½ pound sweet butter
¼ cup egg whites (can add
    more if dough is crumbly)

Mix all ingredients (except sugar) until dough comes together in one lump and pulls away from sides of the bowl. With your hands, form a log-shaped roll that is as thick as your finger. With knife cut pieces about 3 inches long and shape into horseshoes. Bake in 350-degree oven for 12–15 minutes, or until lightly browned. Remove from pan and immediately place in large container with confectioners' sugar (remove vanilla bean). Coat with sugar, then remove to cool. Makes 5 dozen cookies. ✶

An Ocean Liner Christmas—1905

By Lilian C.B. McAlister Mayer

We had a very interesting company on board that Christmas voyage in 1905. There was Mr. Samuel Clemens, bound for Paris, a delightful writer but still more delightful raconteur; Bishop Potter of New York, affable, radiating goodwill toward his fellow passengers; a Japanese gentleman who had come to America to study social and industrial conditions; a young Russian of noble birth; a German baroness with her two beautiful blond children; one of the Krupps of gunmaking fame; an Italian composer who looked like Svengali; and Mr. John Smith of Arizona, reputed to be the owner of three silver mines. These were the notables.

The project of a Christmas entertainment on shipboard met with instant favor. Half the guests volunteered to do something while the captain was more than willing to aid us. He ordered brought from below the holly, bay and fir which had been provided for the dining rooms on Christmas Day and wreaths and festoons and mistletoe converted the long saloon into a real drawing room, homelike and hospitable.

> *The project of a Christmas entertainment on shipboard met with instant favor. Half the guests volunteered to do something while the captain was more than willing to aid us.*

The merriment began in the saloon soon after dinner with Christmas songs of many nations sung by a group of students. Afterward there was a gay informality. Men and women who were utter strangers to each other conversed with the familiarity of friends. Everyone seemed imbued with the spirit of cordiality and good cheer. The only person in the least downcast in that whole assemblage was the young Russian who bemoaned the fact that he was away from home and that there was no one to call him Michael. He had a box of bonbons hung on his door that night with "To Michael" written on it.

Some of the seasick people recovered amazingly, and an old lady of 74 who had not been to a single meal since we started was so carried away by one of Martin Luther's hymns that she joined us and remained all evening, relating some odd Christmas incidents that happened when she was a girl.

The children of the baroness were the life and light of the company. They had made great friends with Mr. Clemens and it was for them that he declined to dance the Virginia reel in order to fulfill his promise to tell them a story. "Not that I don't think a reel a particularly appropriate dance on shipboard," he explained, "but the children come first at Christmastime.

"Now my dears, you know the cows and horses and sheep knew all about the little Christ Child long before the people did, for they were right there and some of them were feeding out of the manger where he lay. So those that knew first told the other animals and there was a great *mooing* and *baaing,* so glad were they that a baby was born who would grow up to be the kindest and best man in the world and who would teach all the people in the world to be kind to each other and to them.

"You know the little song about the cattle lowing and waking the Baby, but it didn't frighten him and he didn't cry at all. That was because he knew the animals were glad he had come into the world and the noises they made were noises of joy to let him know they were happy.

"And so, every Christmas—for this story about the sweet little Babe in the manger has been told to the baby lambs and calves and colts by their mothers each year since then—the animals celebrate his birthday and have the most beautiful time among themselves you can imagine.

"Now when you are in the country at Christmastime you must wake up early and then you will hear them for yourselves and you will know what it all means."

The little ones were much impressed with this story and begged another.

"No," said Mr. Clemens. "Now you must tell one to me."

Editha was shy but Constance came to the rescue bravely:

"Well zen, I'll tell you a nice one. Do you know zat in Germany zere are fairies in Christmas trees? All ze long summer zey fly in ze air and gather ze sunbeams and zey take zem to ze fairy queen and when it gets cold zey build up fires out of zem and keep ze fir trees in ze *wald* green all winter. Isn't zat nice? Did you ever see a real fairy, Mr. Clemens?"

"There are two of them here this very minute," said Mark Twain.

But it was Editha who, as she went off to bed, spoke the wish in all our hearts.

"The good Kris Kringle can't take his reindeer way down in the big ship where it is so hot," she said, "and the men who feed up the fires all the time won't have anything pretty tomorrow. Mother, can't we give something to all the men that work so hard to make the big ship go?"

And then it was decided to remember the men on Christmas morning. One lady further thought of the little children in the steerage, and there was great ransacking of steamer trunks and bags.

As we had no Christmas tree someone suggested we hang up stockings on retiring, after

The next instant a hundred voices caught up the song and the ship resounded with it.

giving all packages into the hands of the stewardess, who would act as Santa Claus. This was successfully carried out, and an officer on watch said the next morning that it was half-ridiculous and half-pathetic to see stockings of every size and color hanging from stateroom doors that night, from a 3-year-old's wee red silk bootie, to the gray half-hose of Mr. Clemens.

Christmas morning dawned cold, with a luminous blue sky and the waves running rose-color from the eastern glow. Even the fashionable folk were up betimes untying boxes and packages. Suddenly a high, pure soprano rang out in the old carol, *O, Come All Ye Faithful.* It was Carl Svenson, the boy soloist of a Boston church who, with his mother, was making a journey to her native Stockholm. The next instant a hundred voices caught up the song and the ship resounded with it. This brought out Bishop Potter, who was exuberant.

"What is the conventional church program compared to this!" he exclaimed. "Why, it's wonderful! It is like the spontaneity of the olden times when carols were sung in the streets on Christmas morning. Go on!" And we did go on, singing every Christmas song, hymn and canticle that came into our heads.

We had a special Christmas service at 11 o'clock and dinner at noon. There were few absentees and everyone looked happy. Our own enjoyment was heightened by the knowledge that the crew to a man had been served with all the extras of the day— turkey, cranberry sauce and other delectable things. ✷

Christmas Memory

By Sharon Fetts

One winter evening not long before Christmas, my daughter, Laurel, and I decided to pay Grandma Smith a visit. This was very easy to do for we lived on the street just south of hers.

As we bundled up to leave, I thought maybe we shouldn't go. The snow was over our boots and the wind was drifting it higher.

When we stepped out into the night, the scene before us took our breath away. Everywhere the snow was shining. It was whirling about the lampposts, catching the light. Before us, behind us, all around us it was circling and glowing as if we were in a snowy fairyland. The path before us was like millions of diamonds.

My 5-year-old looked up with such wonder in her big brown eyes that my own filled with what we call "happy tears."

While we walked the three or so blocks to Grandma's, we kept pointing out familiar objects covered with the glistening snow. As we approached our destination, I thought of how warm and cozy it would be in Grandma's house, and I wondered how much longer God would share her with us. She had aged so fast since Grandpa had died.

As we walked in the front door she didn't come to see who it was for she was busy in the kitchen. We shed our coats and boots and went to watch.

There at the round, wooden kitchen table she was mixing her special sugar cookies. She was just about tuckered out for she mixed them by hand, as she always did.

Seeing the look on my little girl's face as she watched her great-grandmother, I slipped back in time and saw myself watching this same woman making these same cookies.

Grandma and I exchanged smiles and I think she knew what was going through my mind.

She finished mixing the dough and asked me to carry the bowl to the enclosed front porch to chill. Early next morning she would bake them.

We sat down and talked of Christmas just two days away until it was time for us to go. Kisses, smiles, hugs and "See you soon, Grandma." Then out into the snowy night we went, bound for home. Again we remarked on how pretty the snow was and how good the cookie dough had smelled. We got home and soon were snuggled warm in bed.

All this happened three years ago, and now, two years and five months after Grandma's passing, I sit at her kitchen table (which sits in my kitchen now) and write of that snowy magical night.

I thank God for making a wonderful Christmas memory out of such simple things—snow, sugar cookie dough, secret smiles, and the best Grandma a girl ever had. Grandma has passed away but is not forgotten. Grandma and this memory live on.

How do I know?

Because every now and then my 8-year-old comes to me with a starry look in her eyes and says, "Mommie, do you remember that snowy night we walked to Grandma's?"

"Yes, Laurel, I remember and so does Grandma." ✴

CHRISTMAS

At Home

By Loise Pinkerton Fritz

I traveled today on the wings of song,
The wings of a mirthful song.
I hummed, I whistled; my heart rejoiced
As I leisurely strolled along.
I paced wooden floors with round, braided rugs;
I saw on the mantle so high
The old wooden clock that throughout the years
Was still ticking, chiming time.
On windowsills wide, poinsettias bloomed;
Mistletoe hung o'er a door;
A little green wreath was tied to each shade,
Like back in those days of yore.
A fresh-cut fir tree, with angel on top,
Stood in the parlor that day;
'Neath its greens, popcorn-strung,
a manger scene stood …
"Baby Jesus" asleep on the hay.
I traveled today on the wings of song,
The wings of a joyful song.
The lyrics were those of family love
At Christmas … and all year long.
The tune was a tune of sweet harmony
With notes familiar, well-known;
I traveled today on the wings of song
Labeled: "Christmas At Home."